IMAGES
of America

CAMP FORREST

ON THE COVER: Soldiers stationed at Camp Forrest continually trained and practiced combat and tactical maneuvers until each reaction became instinctual. After being inducted, men went through basic training and then, if applicable, to a specialized school for advanced training. Some of the specialized schools taught skills in advanced communication, chemical warfare, and medicine. (National Archives and Records Administration, College Park, Maryland.)

IMAGES
of America

CAMP FORREST

Elizabeth Taylor

ARCADIA
PUBLISHING

ISBN 978-1-4671-1547-6

Published by Arcadia Publishing
Charleston, South Carolina

Printed in the United States of America

Library of Congress Control Number: 2015947050

For all general information, please contact Arcadia Publishing:
Telephone 843-853-2070
Fax 843-853-0044
E-mail sales@arcadiapublishing.com
For customer service and orders:
Toll-Free 1-888-313-2665

Visit us on the Internet at www.arcadiapublishing.com

This book is dedicated to those men and women who trained or worked at Camp Forrest. Words cannot truly express our appreciation to each of you for your dedication to this nation.

Contents

ACKNOWLEDGMENTS

Many individuals helped to compile and compose this brief history of Camp Forrest. Dr. R.B. Rosenburg, Lisa Ramsey, William Greason, Susan Wesley, and Robert Armstrong provided invaluable information and assistance as well as open access to their family heirlooms, for which I am so grateful to them.

Images for this book were compiled from the archives of the CampForrest.com Foundation (CFF); Metro Nashville Archives (MNA); National Archives and Records Administration, Atlanta, Georgia, (NARA-ATL); National Archives and Record Administration, College Park, Maryland, (NARA-CP); Tennessee State Library and Archives (TSLA); and US Army Women's Museum (USAWM); as well as private collections that will be cited individually throughout the text.

INTRODUCTION

Although Camp Forrest was located on the home front, the important role it played in helping the United States win World War II should not be underestimated. Situated in the Cumberland Mountains, Camp Forrest was located on the outskirts of Tullahoma in Middle Tennessee. The cantonment was one of the largest training and induction facilities in the United States and served as the training grounds for infantry, artillery, engineering, and signal divisions. There were approximately 81 different battalions stationed at Camp Forrest at various points throughout the war. The base had its beginnings as Camp Peay, the Tennessee state guard facility.

Tennessee was one of only a few states with both national and state guard units. Built in 1926 and named for then-governor Austin Peay, the state guard facility encompassed over 1,000 acres and accommodated over 2,500 men for annual maneuvers. The facility had sewage amenities, streets, and over 30 buildings, including mess halls, barracks, warehouses, administrative buildings, and several bathhouses. In addition to being used as a state guard facility, sources indicate it also served as temporary housing for refugees from the flood of the Mississippi and Ohio Rivers in 1937 and occasionally as an FBI training facility.

At the onset of World War II and at the behest of Tennessee state officials, the US government appropriated and expanded Camp Peay into a federal Army training and induction base. With the United States becoming drawn into the war in Europe, it became necessary to increase the facilities and to train soldiers at home on a larger scale before sending them to fight overseas. In late 1940, the base was greatly expanded to approximately 85,000 acres. During construction, there was a continual lack of accommodations, food supply shortages, the potential for robbery, and recurrent muddy, frozen, or dry working conditions for the approximately 22,000–28,000 individuals employed there.

It cost approximately $36 million to build the 1,300 buildings, 55 miles of roads, and 5 miles of railroad tracks that Camp Forrest contained. The 1,300 buildings consisted of approximately 408 barracks, 158 mess halls, 14 officer mess buildings, 19 guardhouses, 35 warehouses, 20 administrations buildings, 30 officer quarters buildings, a bakery, an ice plant, an incinerator, a cold storage building, a laundry, a water and sewage treatment facility, a dental clinic, and a 2,000-patient hospital. William Northern Field, an air training base, was located just north of Tullahoma; it was the state's third-largest airfield at the time and served as an Army Air Force training site for B-24 bombers, observation plane pilots, and paratroopers. A model Nazi village was also built on the outskirts of the camp to allow Army Rangers to practice realistic combat training maneuvers.

Camp Forrest employed approximately 12,000 civilians in a variety of jobs on base, including operation of the post exchanges (PXs); a 9,000-square-foot laundry; staffing at the induction center; and vehicle, tank, and artillery maintenance shops. The Tennessee Historical Society reported that over 250,000 soldiers received their initial Army physical exams at Camp Forrest. When not training for war, soldiers had numerous options on base to occupy their time, such as watching a movie at one of the theaters, attending religious services or dinners and dances at the service clubs, checking out reading material at the library, or shopping at the numerous PXs. The surrounding area included a nine-hole golf course, sports arena, gun range, and recreational facilities for archery, swimming, tennis, and bowling. Throughout the war, more than 300 marriages were performed on base. In town, there were five USO clubs, three theaters, a bus station, a railroad station, and a multitude of churches. Soldiers could use a day pass to take a bus or train to Nashville or Chattanooga.

Designed to provide soldiers with a realistic war experience, the Tennessee Maneuvers began throughout the state in June 1941. The region was selected for war game activities because its terrain most closely resembled the European front. Residents became accustomed to soldiers camping out on lawns, continuous construction, and constant maneuvers and training exercises by the various battalions. Gen. George S. Patton's "Hell on Wheels" battalion came from Fort Benning, Georgia, to participate in the maneuvers. Property owners were often forced to seek reparations from the federal government for damages caused by the maneuvers. Livestock also became victims of the war games; the loud noises frequently caused hens to stop laying eggs and cows to stop producing milk.

In 1942, the camp transitioned from a training and induction facility to an enemy alien internment camp, which housed from 200 to more than 800 individuals over the next year. These individuals were transferred to North Dakota in mid-1943, and the facility became a prisoner of war (POW) camp. The first POWs to arrive were approximately 1,500 Germans, and by 1946, an average of 20,480 POWs were held at Camp Forrest. Some POWs were processed and sent to other facilities, while others were permanently "stationed" at Camp Forrest. These POWs served in various roles during their confinement in the camp, including harvesting area crops, processing pulpwood, unloading supplies at train depots, and producing and weaving camouflage nets. POWs were housed in small huts; however, accounts indicate they were poorly insulated, and rain made the grounds continually muddy. These individuals had access to the medical and dental facilities at the camp.

POWs also had access to educational and recreational facilities while at Camp Forrest. The federal government instituted the Intellectual Diversion Program in an attempt to influence German POWs to believe that American culture and people should be appreciated and respected. Initial attempts to gain the confidence of these individuals were not subversive. American officers helped the POWs obtain educational and recreational materials. Initially, correspondence courses were available; later, courses in subjects such as US history, geography, and English were offered at the camp. As time progressed, the POWs put on theatrical productions, started a band/orchestra, and produced a newspaper. POWs were allowed to write home (and to receive cards/letters from home), but the correspondence was generally reviewed by both American and German postal censors looking for codes or hidden messages. Records indicate that 86 POWs died while at Camp Forrest—73 from natural causes, 4 killed in accidents, 1 killed while attempting to escape, 1 killed after attacking a guard, and 7 who committed suicide. There were 30 escape attempts; however, only one POW was killed, and the others were recaptured.

Activities at the camp were drastically reduced after D-Day in France. In 1946, the camp was decommissioned, and its land and buildings were declared surplus. All the buildings were eventually sold as scrap or relocated elsewhere by their respective buyers. In 1951, the lands were recommissioned as Arnold Air Force Base. The 85,000 acres on which Camp Forrest resided is only a portion of the overall Arnold Air Force Base complex. Considered one of the most advanced and largest flight test simulation facilities in the world, the current complex is located on a very small area of the original Camp Forrest site. The only reminders of Camp Forrest are a few decaying chimneys and concrete slabs, as well as impact craters from artillery explosions. When the war ended, the lives and the landscape of Camp Forrest were irrevocably changed.

One

Camp Peay
A Precursor to War

In 1926, Camp Peay was built as a summer training facility for the Tennessee National Guard, 181st Field Artillery Regiment. The Nashville, Chattanooga & St. Louis Railroad donated the initial land for the facility. Tennessee was one of the first states to have its own state military division. (CFF.)

The 1,040-acre Camp Peay cantonment was located east of Tullahoma. It consisted of approximately 22 buildings, including an administrative building, a warehouse, a garage, an emergency airfield, kitchens and mess halls, bathhouses, and a stable. The facility also had a water tower, a sewage and water system, and several paved roads. (CFF.)

This aerial view of Camp Peay shows the size of the cantonment, which also served as a training facility for FBI field maneuvers and as temporary housing for approximately 1,500 African American refugees from the 1937 flood of the Mississippi and Ohio Rivers. These individuals were primarily sharecroppers and tenant farmers from the lowland sections of Tennessee, Arkansas, and Mississippi. (MNA.)

Tennessee governor Austin Peay held office from 1923 to 1927. He reformed many elements of the ailing state government and was soon able to boast of a surplus in the state's coffers. Some of his more notable accomplishments include state administrative reform, improvements to the secondary education system, expansions of the road system, and the creation of the Great Smoky Mountains National Park. (TSLA.)

Prentice Cooper was governor of Tennessee from 1939 to 1945, following a successful law career and terms in the state senate and house of representatives. After a trip to Germany, Cooper began readying his state, as he felt entry into the war was imminent. The World War I veteran organized the Tennessee State Defense Council, established a draft board, prepared the state guard for the country's entrance into World War II, and attracted large defense-related industries. (TSLA.)

This 1936 photograph shows the men from the Tennessee National Guard Headquarters Company, 2nd Battalion, 117th Infantry Regiment, during summer training exercises at Camp Peay. This regiment was attached to the 30th Infantry Division ("Old Hickory") during World War II. From left to right are (first row) unidentified, Newton Kile, Robert H. Easterly, William Harmond, Tom Woodrow Pippenger, Don Johnson, Walter ?, unidentified, Walter Link, Earl Link, Nathan Rawlins, and Ray Gamble; (second row) 1st Lt. Charles F. Kelly, Lt. Charles P. Carroll, Sgt. Charles F. Foster, unidentified, Bill W. Bryant, Ben Morrow, four unidentified, Clyde Arter Colloms, three unidentified, and Elgie J. Stone. (Southeast Tennessee Digital Archive [SETDA], Cleveland State Community College.)

Horses and mules were a mainstay at Camp Peay, as the state guard units were still horse-mounted cavalry divisions. By World War II, cavalry divisions had transitioned to mechanized artillery units. In the early months of Camp Forrest, horses and mules moved artillery until the arrival of vehicles. The illustration on this postcard shows soldiers assisted by mules transporting equipment, likely from camp to artillery practice fields. (CFF.)

Several stables were located on the Camp Peay cantonment. Horses mainly provided important logistical support during World War I; however, many were killed on the front by artillery fire, poison gas, starvation, or disease. The constant losses, lack of replacements, and advancement in war machines—such as machine guns and tanks—rendered traditional cavalry units obsolete. The need for horses waned at Camp Forrest as various militarized vehicles became available. (CFF.)

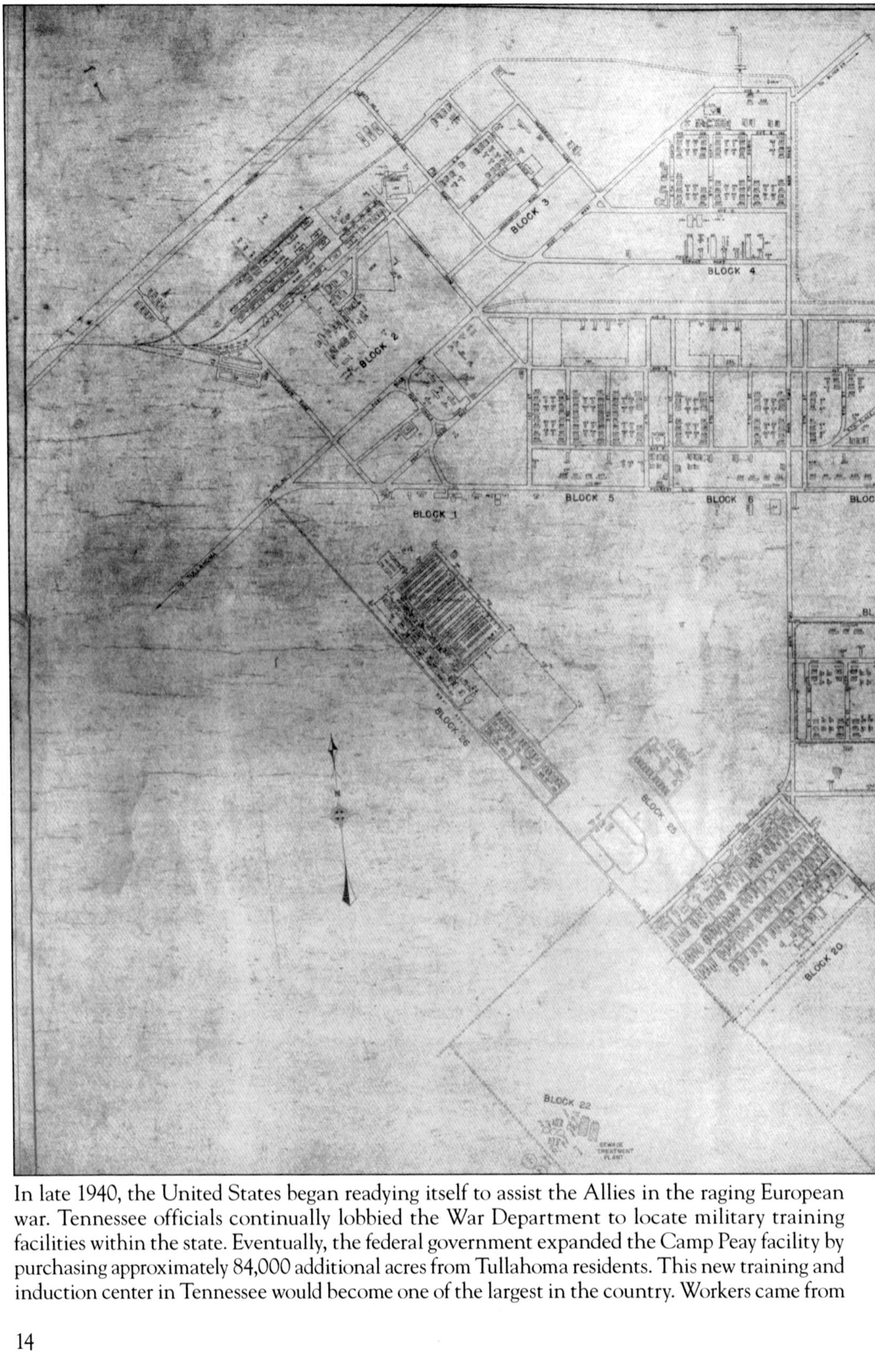

In late 1940, the United States began readying itself to assist the Allies in the raging European war. Tennessee officials continually lobbied the War Department to locate military training facilities within the state. Eventually, the federal government expanded the Camp Peay facility by purchasing approximately 84,000 additional acres from Tullahoma residents. This new training and induction center in Tennessee would become one of the largest in the country. Workers came from

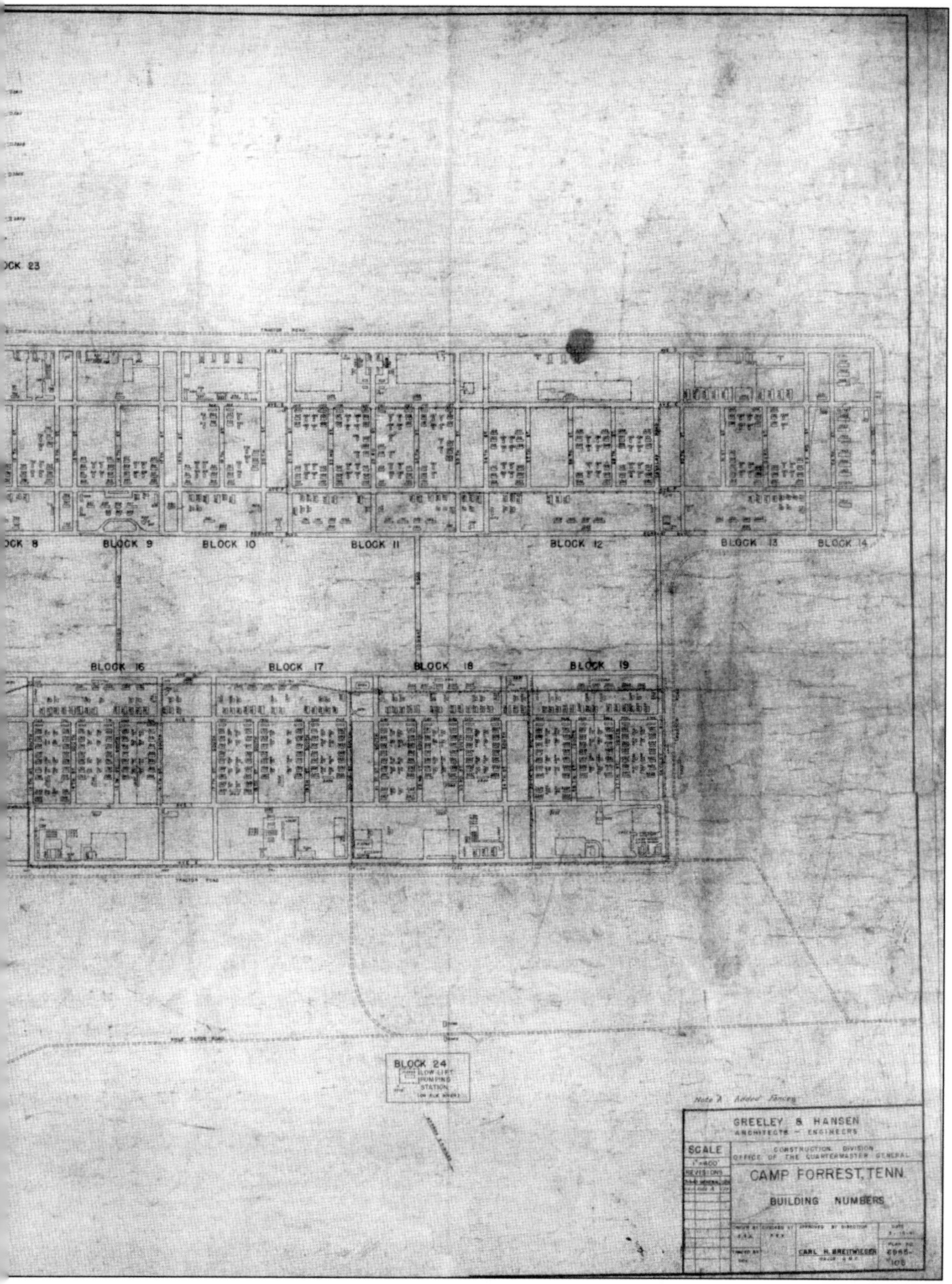

across the nation in search of employment opportunities during the construction phase and once the facility was operational. Over 20,000 individuals were employed at peak construction times. The expansion and upgrade to the existing facility cost approximately $45 million. The facility provided training for infantry, artillery, engineering, and signal organizations. (NARA-ATL.)

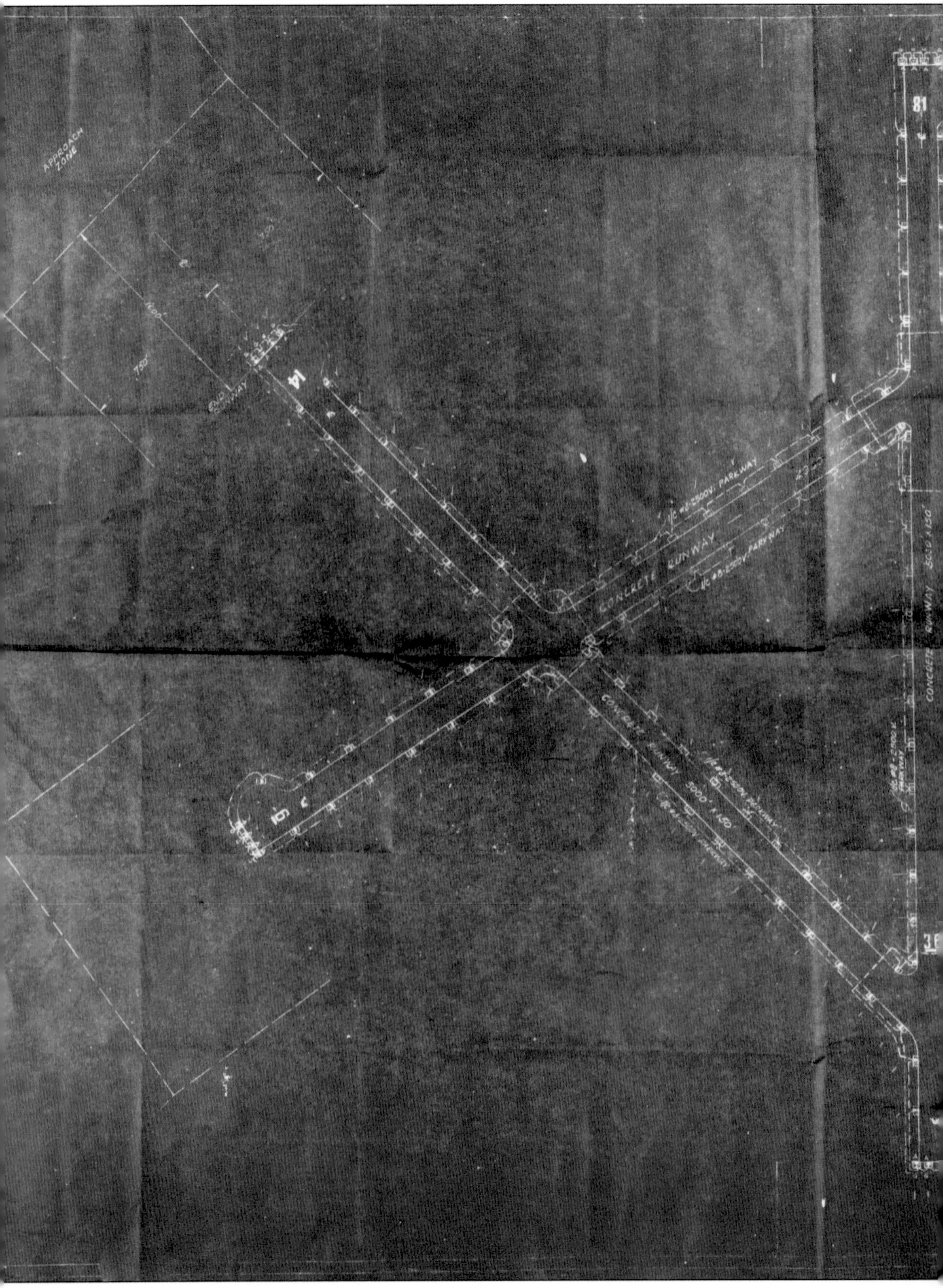
APPROACH ZONE
CONCRETE RUNWAY
CONCRETE RUNWAY 5000' x 150
CONCRETE RUNWAY 5000' x 150
14
18
36

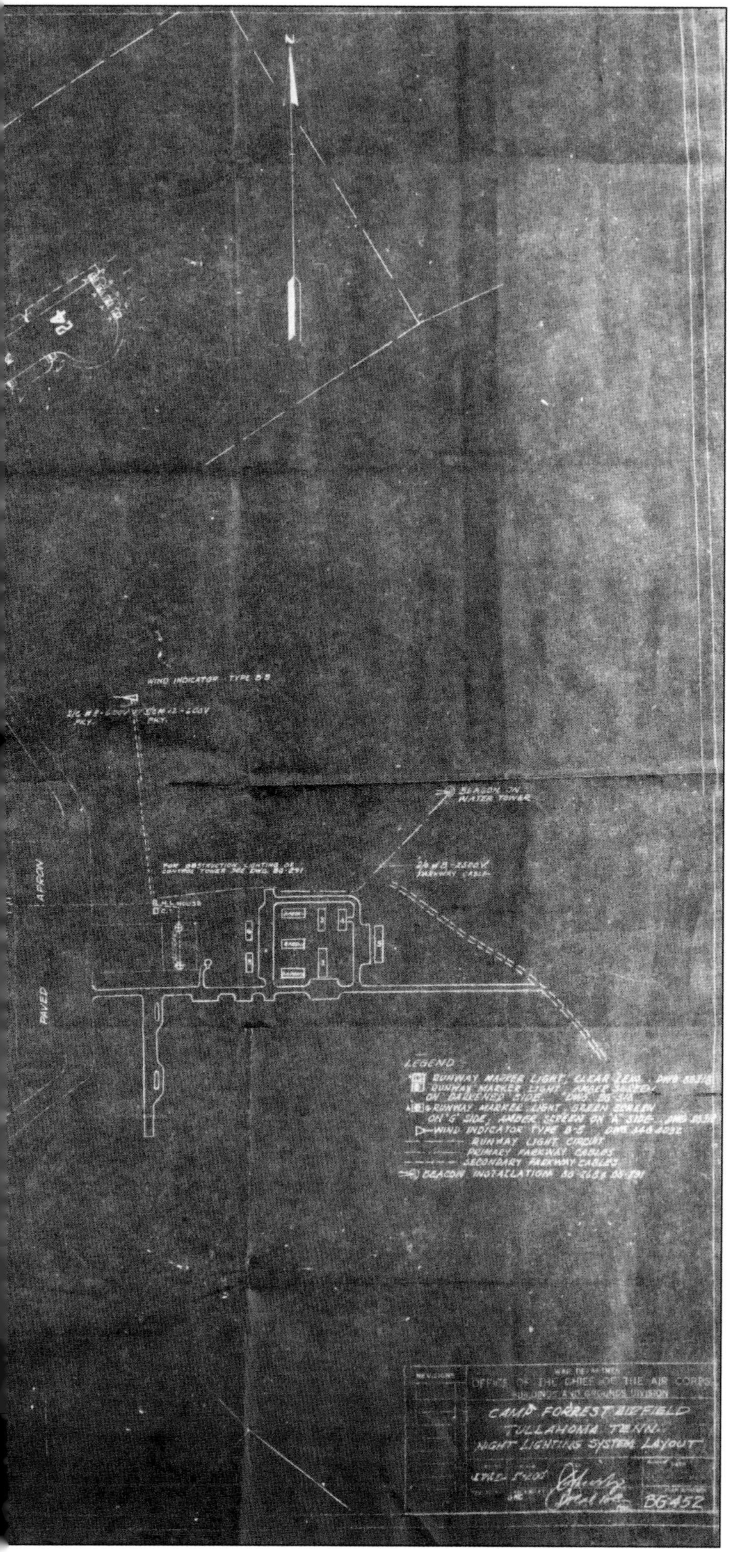

Tullahoma Army Air Base was situated on 1,300 acres about 1.5 miles from Tullahoma. The field contained approximately 100 buildings and three 5,000-foot runways. The facility was designed to accommodate heavy aircraft, such as four-engine B-24 bombers. Numerous Army Air Force units, including pilot, paratrooper, and glider trainees, used this aircraft throughout the war. The facility's name was changed to William Northern Field in November 1942 to honor the first Tennessee pilot killed in the war. It was the third-largest airfield in Tennessee. Many of the original buildings were dismantled as surplus at the conclusion of World War II. Currently, the area is home to the Beechcraft Heritage Museum and the Tullahoma Regional Airport. (NARA-ATL.)

When Camp Peay became federalized in 1940, its name was subsequently changed to Camp Forrest. Amid much protest, the War Department elected to stand firm in its decision to honor one of the Civil War's most celebrated and controversial Confederate cavalry leaders, Gen. Nathan Bedford Forrest. The Tennessee native was infamous for committing Civil War crimes and being a founding member of the Ku Klux Klan. (TSLA.)

Two

CAMP FORREST
PREPARATION FOR WAR

The 33rd Division from Illinois was one of the first divisions to arrive at Camp Forrest in the spring of 1941. Reports indicated trains ran day and night as inductees began arriving for yearlong training. There were typically no fewer than 70,000 troops throughout the area between 1942 and 1944. (CFF.)

While most of the buildings at Camp Forrest were completed when troops began arriving, there were still unfinished construction projects, such as installing raised sidewalks, insulating the insides of barracks, filling in stump holes, and leveling the parade field. Many of the battalions assisted with these projects when they were not training. (CFF, photograph by Robert "Bob" Laughlin Couch Jr.)

The headquarters building housed many of the division offices, such as quartermaster, judge advocate security, signal, intelligence, financial, engineering, and general administration. There were approximately 20 different administrative buildings throughout the camp. Maj. Gen. Samuel T. Lawton served as commanding officer of Camp Forrest, and Col. Horace Thornton was chief of staff. Under their direction, numerous divisions sought to ensure daily operations were efficient and effective. (CFF.)

The base was a self-sustaining city that did not require external sources of power, water, sewage, or other utilities. There was also a railroad spur that brought troops and supplies directly into the camp. During the height of the war years, the camp became the fifth-largest city in the state of Tennessee. Reports indicate that an estimated 250,000 troops and 22,000 POWs passed through the facility. (TSLA.)

Along Camp Forrest's roads were over 1,300 buildings, including approximately 535 barracks, 158 mess halls, 168 day halls, 22 warehouses, 11 chapels, 4 theaters, a 1,000-bed hospital, a sports arena, 22 filling stations, 2 service clubs, and a headquarters. There were also 10 miles of paved roads and 15 miles of gravel roads. (CFF.)

The base was equipped with a fully operational water plant, as well as a sewage treatment and disposal facility. Newspapers of the time reported that the water system could accommodate a city of 30,000 inhabitants. Water was drawn from a pumping station at the Elk River before traveling four miles via 20-inch pipes to the camp's center. (CFF.)

Rows of warehouses that contained items such as food supplies, weapons, ammunitions, and clothing were located throughout the camp. The quartermaster division was responsible for the procurement, storage, and disbursement of supplies on the home front and the war front. Supplies and materials were obtained from a diverse set of suppliers at both local and national levels. (CFF.)

Rain transformed the red Tennessee clay into muddy quagmires. The mud was especially problematic during construction, as men and machines could become mired down in the sticky muck. Once troops arrived, raised sidewalks were built to allow for easy access to and from main roads and the various buildings throughout the camp. (CFF.)

Troops set up encampments in surrounding fields when the base barracks were full. During the winter months, men would huddle inside the pup tents with lit candles in an effort to stay warm. Maj. Gen Samuel T. Lawton generally encouraged division commanders to create realistic living conditions for the troops in an effort to prepare them for the trials and tribulations that lay ahead. (TSLA.)

Once clothes were cleaned at the quartermaster laundry, they were wrapped in paper and returned to their owners. The laundry was the largest civilian employer on base and could clean approximately 55,000 pounds of clothes per day. At the wrapping table are Dolly Brewer (left) of Winchester, Tennessee, and Laura LaPointe (right) of Tullahoma, Tennessee. (NARA-CP.)

Laundry services were an essential component of base life, as each soldier was expected to maintain a neat and well-groomed appearance at all times. At the 9,000-square-foot laundry facility, Helen Maxwell of Tullahoma, Tennessee, marked clothes as they were brought in for cleaning. The clothes were individually marked in an effort to ensure each garment was returned to the correct owner. (NARA-CP.)

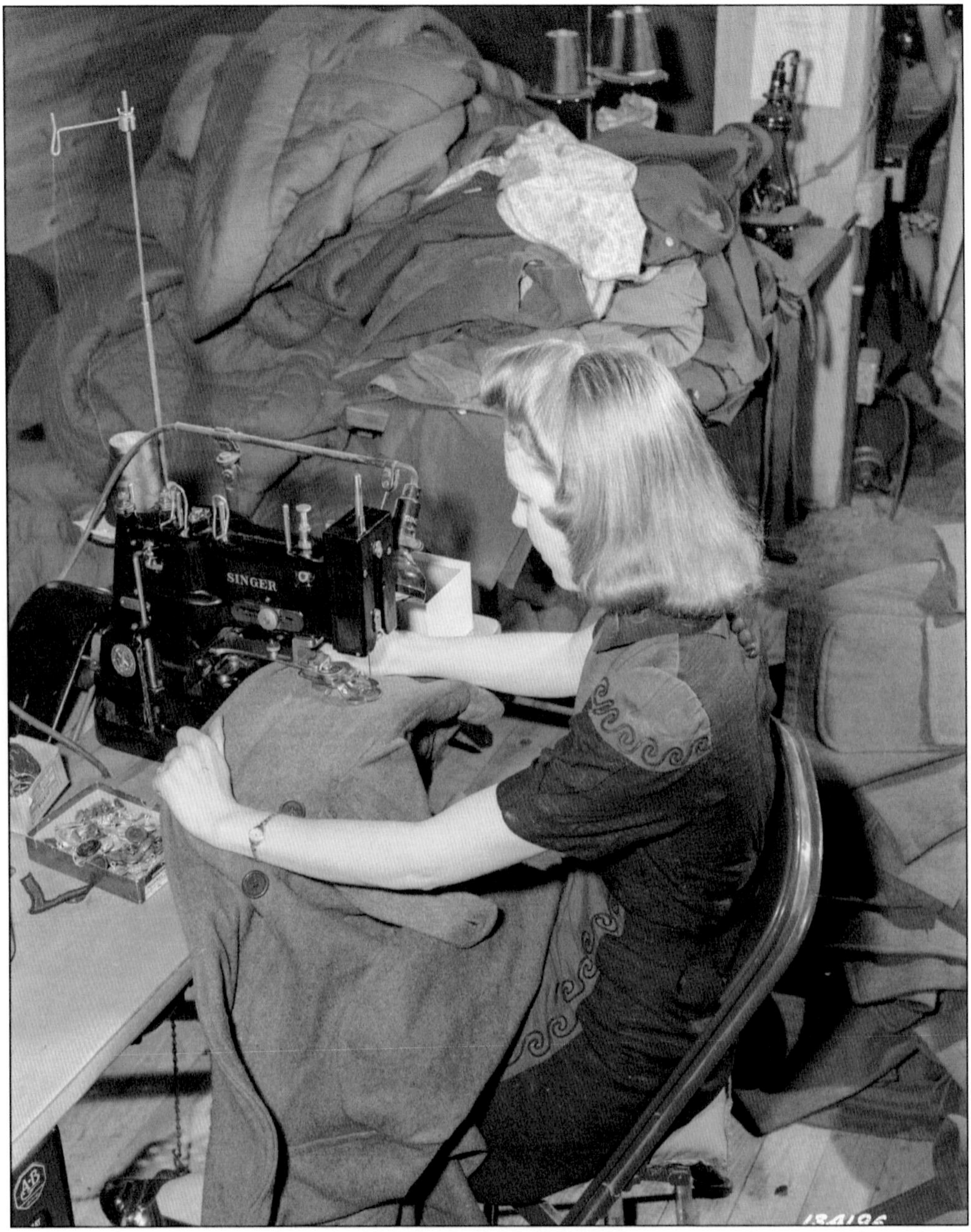

The clothing and equipment repair shop was responsible for repairing uniforms and shoes that a soldier had returned to the quartermaster division as being damaged. To keep waste to a minimum, any item found to be beyond repair was recycled for another purpose, such as cleaning rags. In this photograph, Madilen Brown of Shelbyville, Tennessee, sews buttons on a soldier's overcoat. (NARA-CP.)

Although soldiers were taught how to care for their footwear, countless hours of marching eventually wore down the shoe leather. On the home front, inductees could have shoes patched at the clothing and equipment repair shop. Overseas, a mobile shoe repair shop was able to quickly mend footwear. Here, Cecil C. Centrew of McMinnville, Tennessee, repairs a soldier's shoes. (NARA-CP.)

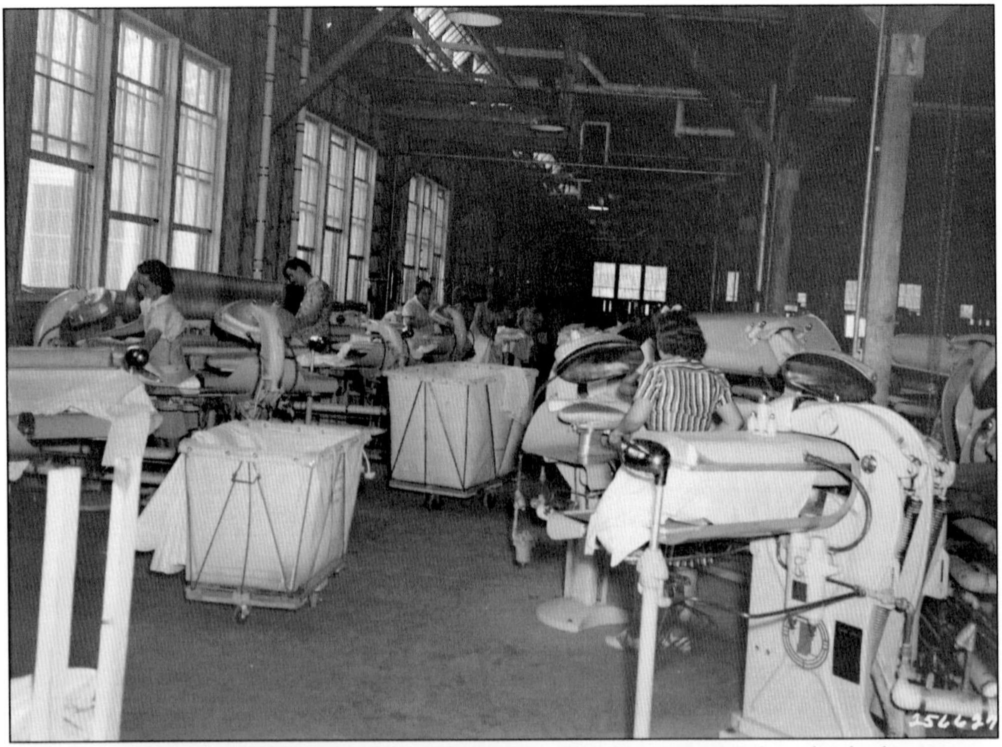

The Camp Forrest laundry facility was considered one of the largest single-floor dry cleaning operations within the state. It was equipped with a large boiler, water softening plant, numerous washers and dryers, small pressing machines, and flatwork presses. It was operational from 1941 until the base closed. As the camp transitioned into a POW facility, many German soldiers worked in the laundry. (NARA-CP.)

The Finance Department ensured requisitions were paid on time. (Susan Wesley.)

Col. Ira Summers (left) of Chattanooga, Tennessee, was commanding officer of the 181st Field Artillery, and Brig. Gen. Raymond Yenter (right) of Des Moines, Iowa, was commander of the 75th Brigade. They are shown here discussing military plans. The planning of daily operations throughout the camp was an immense undertaking, as it served to coordinate the training for infantry, artillery, engineer, and signal divisions. (MNA.)

Capt. James N. Freeman (left) of Nashville, Tennessee, was the left adjunct of the 181st Field Artillery, and Lt. Col. Paul Jordan (right) of Chattanooga, Tennessee, was the executive officer of the 181st Field Artillery. This division—part of the Tennessee National Guard—was federalized in February 1941. Other divisions stationed alongside the 181st include the 168th Field Artillery, Colorado National Guard; and the 33rd Infantry Division, Illinois National Guard. (MNA.)

Administrative duties for divisions, such as the Quartermaster Corps, required a dedicated support staff to ensure operations were continually managed efficiently and effectively. When processing requisitions for equipment, supplies, clothing, and food, the paperwork was typed in triplicate. Here, the men of Company B, 95th Signal Battalion, are honing their skills using both manual typewriters and Teletype machines. (NARA-CP.)

At the start of World War II, the US Army Corps of Engineers was responsible for fire protection on army bases. The war saw the creation of engineer firefighting detachments, which were responsible, in part, for combating fires overseas. Military firefighting schools in Louisiana provided specialized training before men were deployed. Pictured is one of the fire trucks at Camp Forrest. (Lisa Ramsey.)

The base fire station was staffed with two chiefs and 26 firefighters, both military and civilian. Firefighters had to be ready to put out fires that might erupt from discharged weapons, kitchen accidents, or general carelessness. The most common fire engine at World War II military bases had a 150-gallon water tank and 1,000 feet of hose. (Lisa Ramsey.)

The Nashville, Chattanooga & St. Louis Railway provided the area's train service. However, the station, which was located in the center of town, was too small and continually created traffic jams due to the large number of troops arriving each day. To alleviate the problem, a larger station was built several blocks from the city center in Tullahoma. This troop just disembarked from the train at Camp Forrest. (MNA.)

Most of the troops arrived at Camp Forrest by train from destinations throughout the United States. Pictured is one of the Women's Army Corps (WAC) units stationed on the Tennessee base. These women joined the military to support the war effort but were routinely regulated to more minimal tasks, such as sweeping warehouses, working in post exchanges (PXs) or cafeterias, or handling secretarial duties. (USAWM.)

TSgt. Charles W. Barbour was in charge of the camp bakery. Here, he is placing finished loaves of freshly baked bread in a specially constructed sanitary bread box for shipment to camp mess halls. In February 1941, the *Chicago Tribune* reported that soldiers were trained in general cooking theories as well as learning specific techniques for peeling potatoes and boiling an egg. (NARA-CP.)

Food preparation and safe handling practices became a heightened public health concern during the war years, as greater numbers of soldiers and civilians ate outside of the home. Regulations required specific practices in the handling and preparation of meals on base; however, stringent requirements such as those utilized today were nonexistent in the 1940s. With the ever-increasing population, the Tennessee Department of Health organized a district health department to address these ongoing concerns within the areas surrounding the base. Even the preparation of a meal for a soldier or defense plant worker was deemed important in aiding the war effort. Above is the dining area in one of the many mess halls on base. Below, two recruits on KP (kitchen police) duty are manually peeling potatoes (Above, MNA; below, Susan Wesley.)

F.J. Boles (left), of the National Livestock and Meat Board in Chicago, Illinois, looks on as S.Sgt. R.F. Hill of Sumatra, Florida, cuts meat as part of the training process at the School for Bakers and Cooks at Camp Forrest. Responsibility for such programs fell to the Office of Quartermaster General's Food Service Program, which was charged with ensuring that high food-service standards were continually maintained throughout the Army. (NARA-CP.)

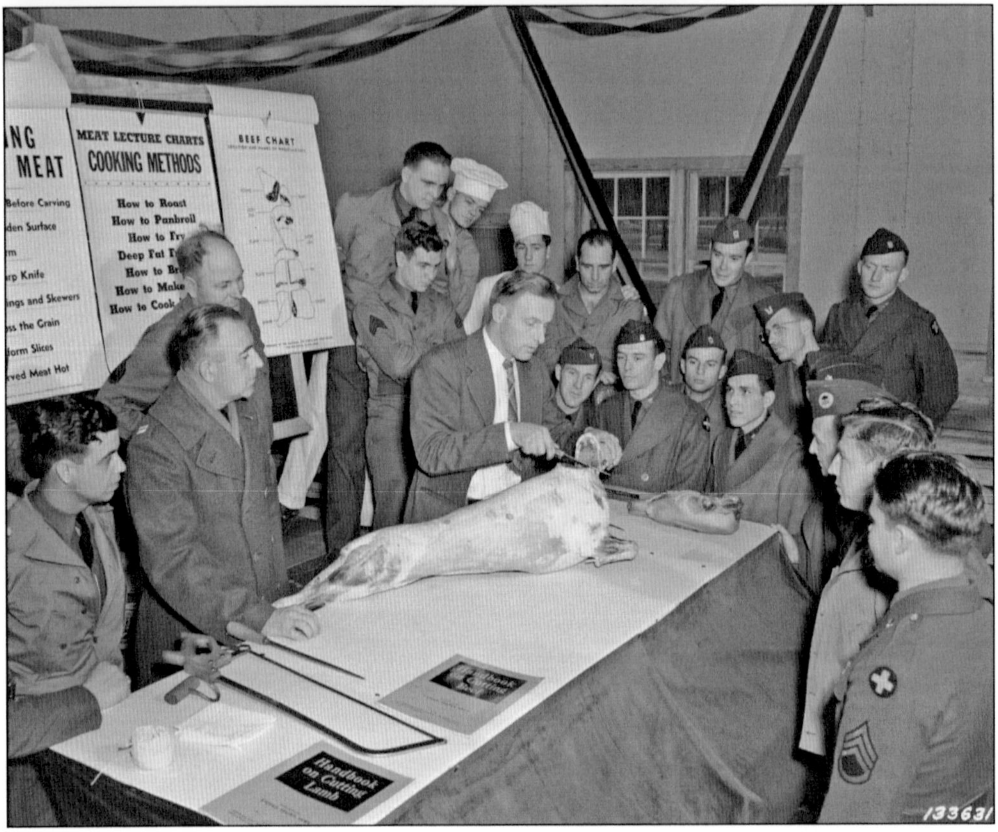

Mess officers and sergeants at the School for Bakers and Cooks receive instruction from F.J. Boles, a representative from the National Livestock and Meat Board. Although military personnel were trained in appropriate food-handling practices, there were no standardized best practices within the private sector. (NARA-CP.)

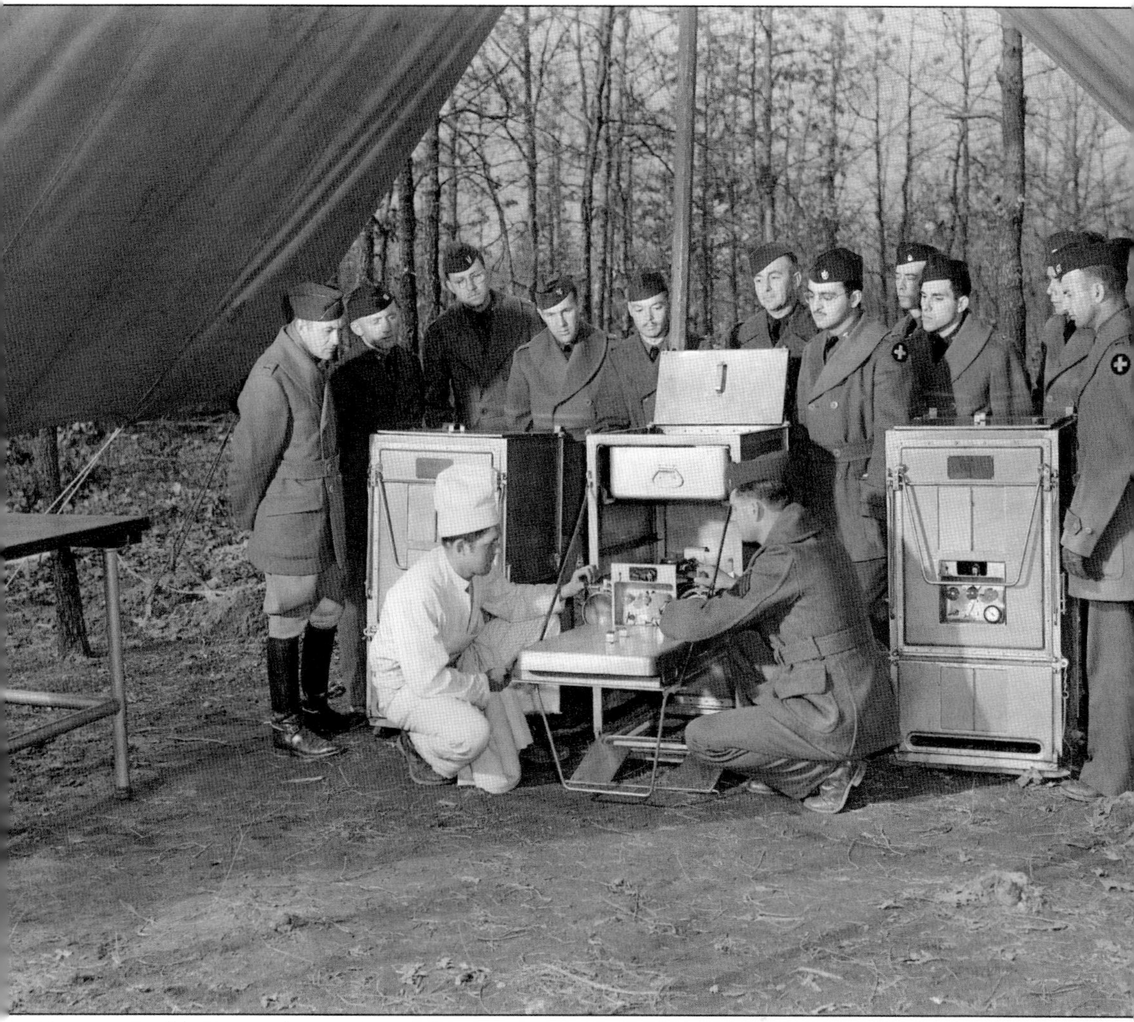

During World War II, the gasoline field range was the newest piece of field cooking equipment. All the cooking utensils, pots, and pans could be stored in the stove for easy movement of the entire apparatus. The men pictured around the stove are, in no specific order, 1st Lt. P.A. Kelly (Kansas City, Missouri), 2nd Lt. J.W. Sitchfield (Toluca, Illinois), 2nd Lt. C.T. Church (Chicago, Illinois), 2nd Lt. J.D. Porter (Chicago, Illinois), 2nd Lt. W.G. Knight (Denver, Colorado), 1st Lt. A.W. Feldman (Chicago, Illinois), 2nd Lt. R.A. Hartlieb (Columbus, Ohio), 2nd Lt. R.S. Ford (Mount Vernon, Illinois), and 1st Lt. L.L. Deckner (Salem, Illinois), Capt. Charles C. Stewart (School for Bakers and Cooks), 1st Lt. G.I. Weatherly Jr. (kneeling; Fort Payne, Alabama), Cook H.L. Sparks (kneeling; Salyersville, Kentucky), and Sgt. R.N. Armstrong (Huntsville, Alabama). (NARA-CP.)

Several different mobile machine shops were used on the home front and overseas throughout World War II for artillery repair, instrument repair, welding, signal repair, and small arms repair. A mobile machine shop was generally equipped with drill presses, lathes, shapers, and hand tools that could machine parts quickly while in the field. (Lisa Ramsey.)

In 1941, Chrysler halted vehicle production and was contracted to produce .45-caliber cartridges for the military at its Indiana plant. Making bullets was a long process, requiring approximately 48 different steps from start to finish. Additionally, a cartridge had to pass approximately 334 quality-control inspections. These soldiers are packing bullets for use in machine guns. (Lisa Ramsey.)

Civilians learned to contend with the adversities that resulted from the base and military maneuvers. For example, units would construct communication lines wherever it was deemed necessary, even if it meant placing lines in the middle of a plowed field or cow pasture. Here, Pvt. Edward Wika (standing on the ground) passes a 10-pin crossarm to Sgt. Virgil Bents as they construct telephone lines at Camp Forrest. (NARA-CP.)

Pvt. Fred Stellpslug and Pvt. Othur New worked to run telephone wire throughout the camp. The lines were tied to insulators after the proper tension had been placed on the lines. (NARA-CP.)

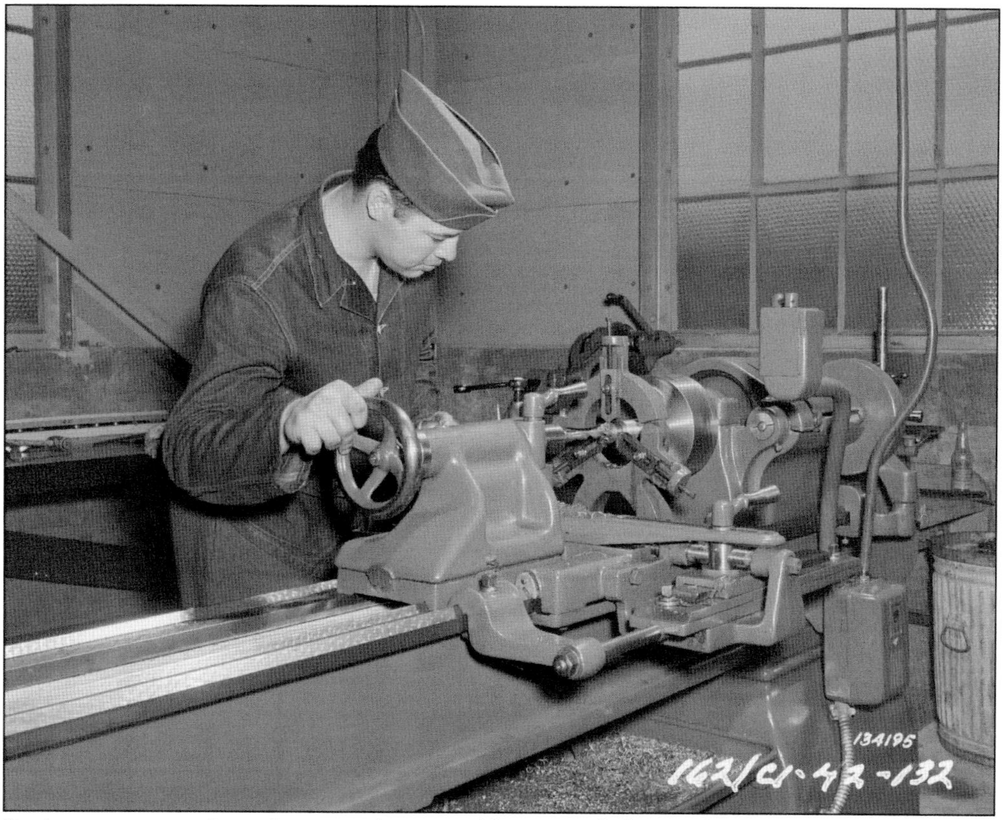

Replacement parts for military machines could not simply be purchased at the local hardware or auto parts store. A base machine shop tooled parts for vehicles and weapons when it was not feasible to use a mobile machine shop. Here, Cpl. Joseph S. Wyrostek, of the 4th Georgia Service Command Ordnance Detachment, machines steel on a medium lathe at the ordnance workshop. (NARA-CP.)

Camp Forrest had a fully functional garage used to service and repair the many military vehicles used on a daily basis. Some of the military vehicles that required repairs included jeeps, passenger carriers, tanks, tractors, trucks, and motorcycles. These vehicles had to be quickly repaired and returned to service. (NARA-CP.)

Soldiers and civilians were employed to maintain the numerous and diverse types of vehicles. Civilians were necessary to assist in filling many of these positions, since troops were sometimes called upon to guard places on American soil. Some of these places included Tennessee Valley Authority (TVA) dams, power lines, bridges, aluminum plants, and other defense plants. (NARA-CP.)

The 1,000-bed hospital at Camp Forrest had a modern operating room, pharmacy, X-ray room, minor outpatient treatment facility, specialty women's clinic, and dental clinic. Dr. Col. Horace E. Thornton was the hospital's chief of staff. The men and women who staffed the hospital not only treated sick and injured soldiers at the base, they were also preparing themselves to later treat the fallen on the battlefield. (CFF.)

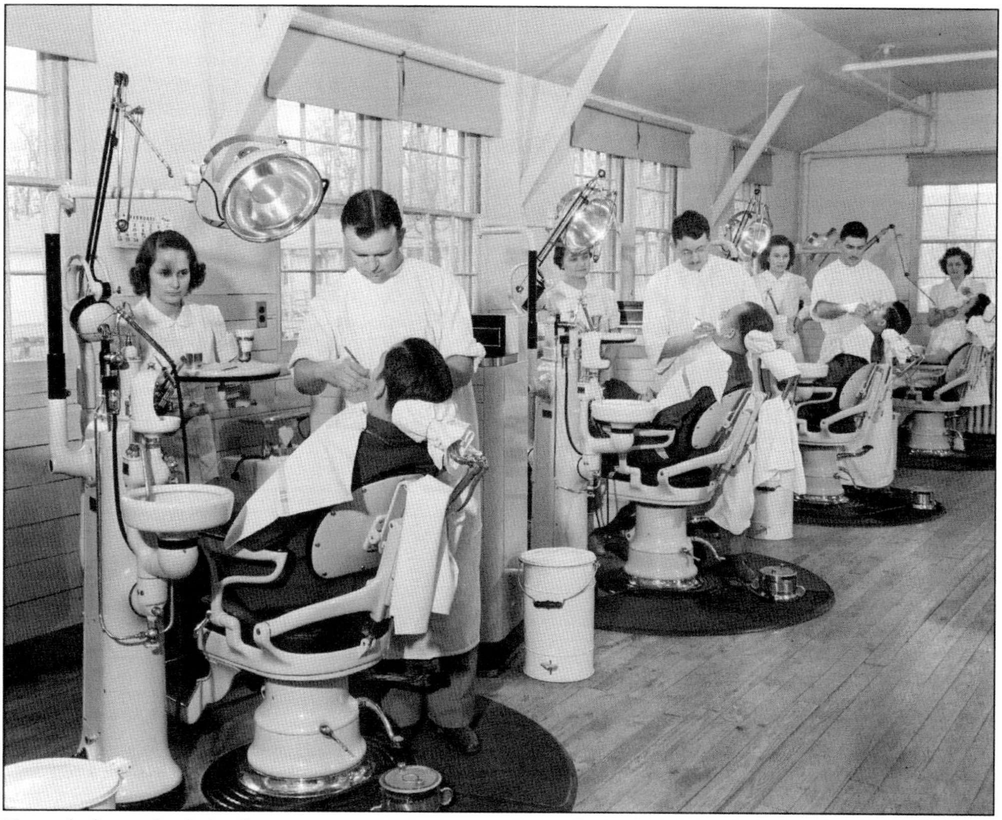

Dental clinics had the latest equipment to ensure satisfactory oral health. From left to right are Jean Malone (Macy, Idaho), S.Sgt. Dennis Wright (Villa Park, Illinois), Capt. Fred Jones (Memphis, Tennessee), Mrs. Valentine Foster (Shelbyville, Tennessee), Lt. G.D. Flaxman (Chicago, Illinois), Pvt. Ralph Surcey (Johnson City, Tennessee), Mrs. A.J. Smith (Chattanooga, Tennessee), Lt. Bernard Lewiston (Chicago, Illinois), Cpl. W.A. McClellan (Nashville, Georgia), Ethel Carter (Nashville, Tennessee), and Ruth Lewis (Wilkes-Barre, Pennsylvania). (NARA-CP.)

The hospital pharmacy was staffed by both military and civilian personnel and dispensed a variety of medicines for patients. From left to right are Will H. Hardman (Puliski, Tennessee), Pvt. Edmund Cherry (Hazel, Kentucky), H.W. Fly (Shelbyville, Tennessee), and Pvt. Theodore Poninak (Milwaukee, Wisconsin). (NARA-CP.)

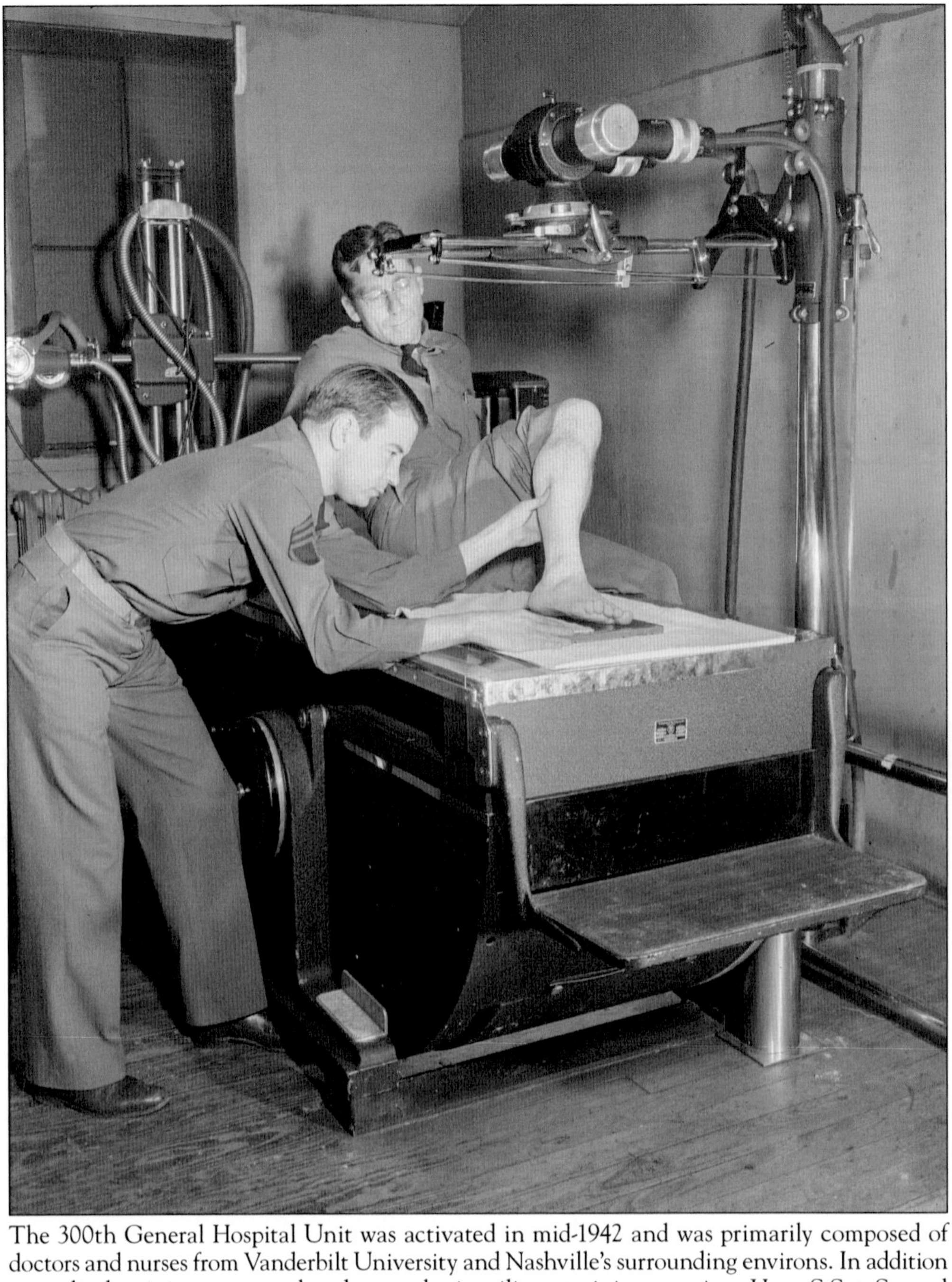

The 300th General Hospital Unit was activated in mid-1942 and was primarily composed of doctors and nurses from Vanderbilt University and Nashville's surrounding environs. In addition to medical training, personnel underwent basic military training exercises. Here, S.Sgt. Samuel C. Deveraux of Nashville, Tennessee, readies Pvt. Gerald W. Teagarden of Chicago, Illinois, for a foot X-ray at the station hospital. (NARA-CP.)

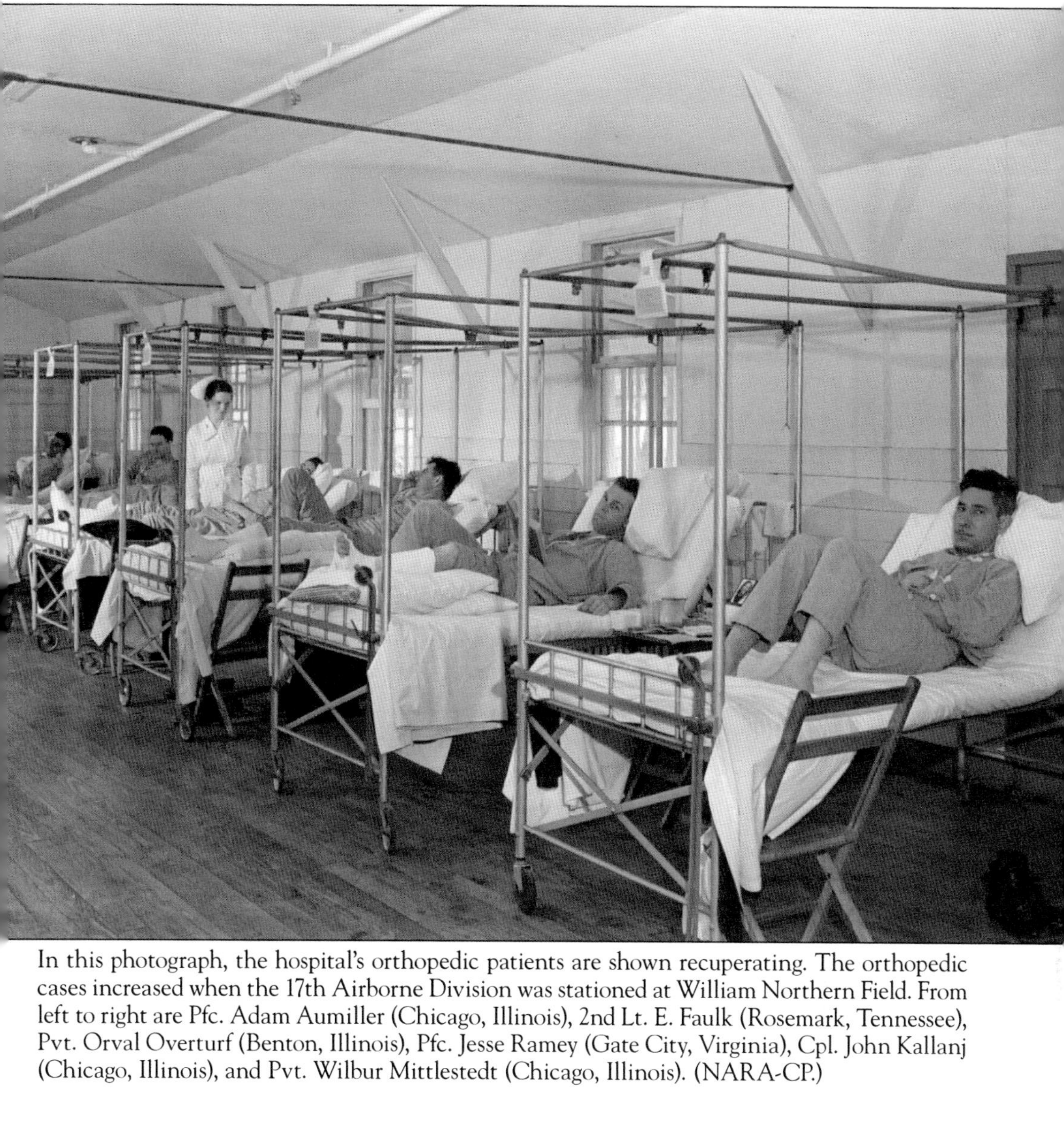

In this photograph, the hospital's orthopedic patients are shown recuperating. The orthopedic cases increased when the 17th Airborne Division was stationed at William Northern Field. From left to right are Pfc. Adam Aumiller (Chicago, Illinois), 2nd Lt. E. Faulk (Rosemark, Tennessee), Pvt. Orval Overturf (Benton, Illinois), Pfc. Jesse Ramey (Gate City, Virginia), Cpl. John Kallanj (Chicago, Illinois), and Pvt. Wilbur Mittlestedt (Chicago, Illinois). (NARA-CP.)

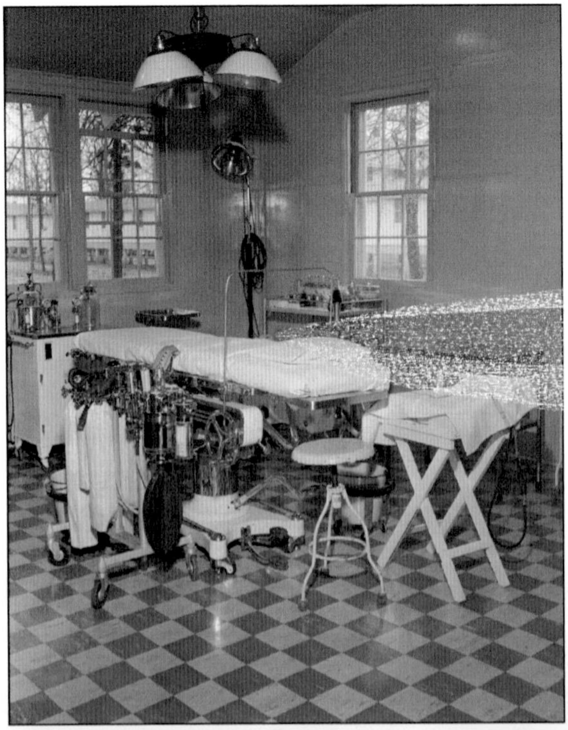

There were approximately 68 buildings in the hospital complex at Camp Forrest. Hospitals that were erected overseas were not as expansive, but they could treat wounds and perform surgery. Soldiers with wounds were treated and returned to the war zone. The overseas hospitals were protected under the Geneva Convention and could be easily identified by the "GC" signage throughout the encampment. (NARA-CP.)

News stories of the day reported on the wonderful care patients received while hospitalized at Camp Forrest. Those convalescing had meals, medicines, and magazines brought to them throughout the day. This photograph shows a patient being moved from a gurney to an operating table at the station hospital. (NARA-CP.)

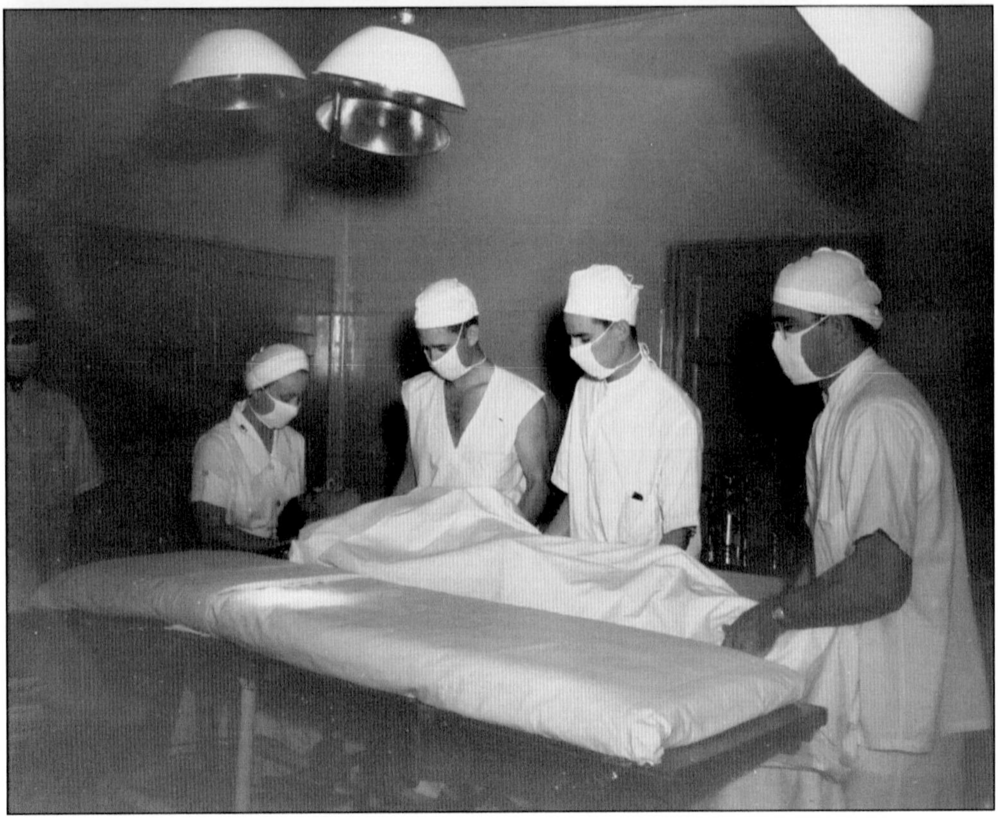

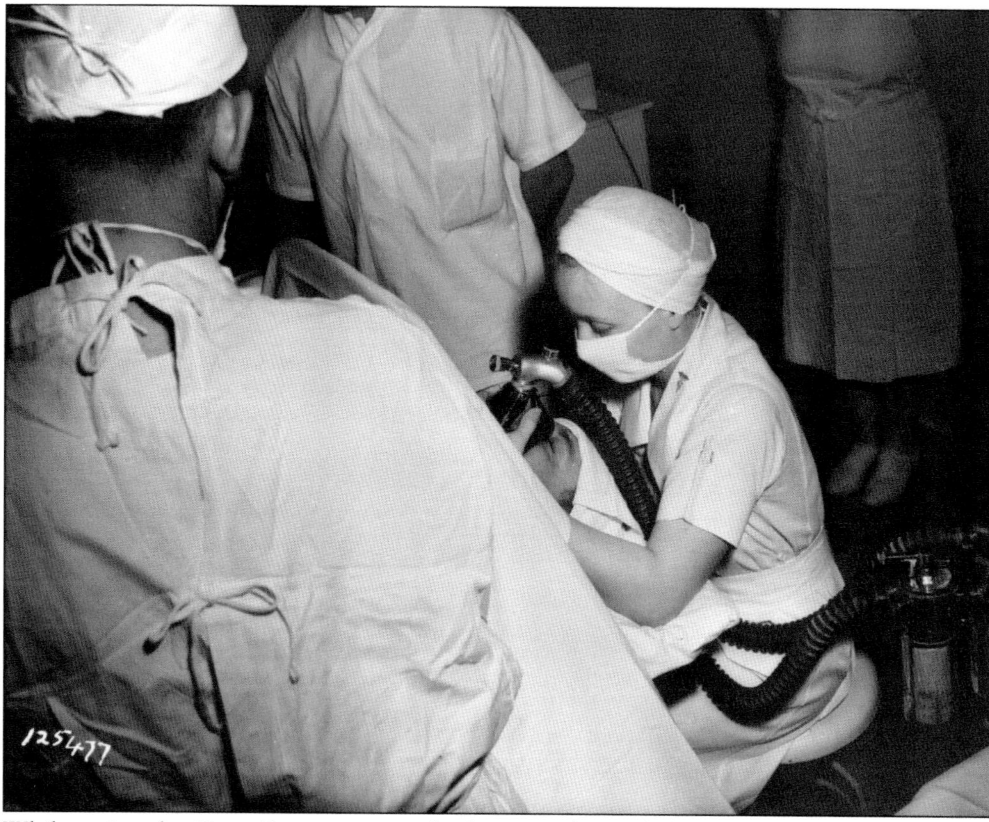

While stationed at Camp Forrest, some medical personnel attended specialized schools for advanced clinical training. In the hospital, wards were cleaned twice a day, and medical personnel were on duty around the clock to care for patients. If medical operations became necessary, the facility was equipped with every modern necessity to ensure that patients received the best possible care. Uncle Sam wanted to ensure men were healthy before sending them off to war. Above, a nurse is administering anesthetic before surgery. Below, a surgery is being performed at Camp Forrest. (Both, NARA-CP.)

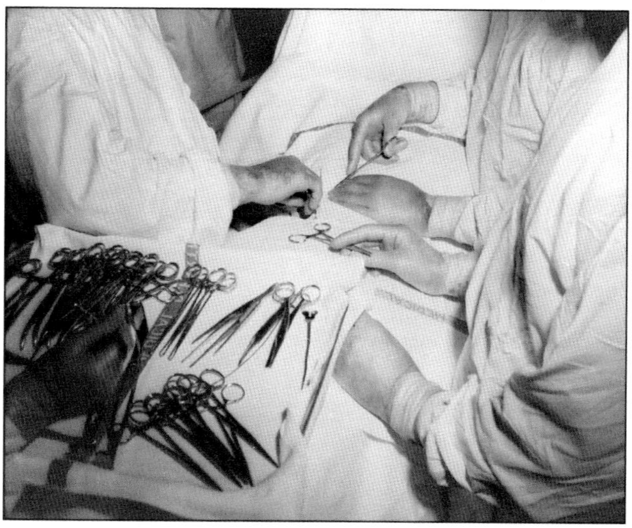

Col. Hew McMurdo was the camp surgeon and commander of the station hospital. The hospital was not limited to treating soldiers. Numerous children were born at Camp Forrest throughout its time as an induction and training facility. While the exact number of births specifically at Camp Forrest is unavailable, there were 6,157 births in Coffee and Franklin Counties from 1941 to 1946. (NARA-CP.)

The station hospital officially opened in March 1941 and had received over 1,100 patients by the end of that month. Despite supply and personnel shortages at the beginning, all hospital services were fully operational by June 1941. Soldiers with minor ailments were typically treated at the Special Troops Dispensary (pictured) rather than the hospital. (NARA-CP.)

Three

WAR MACHINES
WORLD WAR II WEAPONS ON THE FRONT

Although generally thought of as the preferred weapon of gangsters, the Thompson submachine gun was also used on the battlefield. It could be fired from a standing, kneeling, or sitting position, and 20- and 50-round clips gave soldiers the ability to quickly disperse .45-caliber bullets at advancing enemies. (NARA-CP.)

Medium tanks, as shown here, were used throughout the simulated war game maneuvers. The Tennessee Maneuvers occurred over a 21-county area in the state for approximately four years. Accounts suggest that approximately 500,000 combat soldiers and 100,000 support troops participated in preparation for the impending invasion of Europe. (CFF.)

Members of an armored tank division stand beside an M4 Sherman tank (named after Civil War general William T. Sherman) during field maneuvers. Property damage was common, as Gen. George Patton urged his troops to traverse fields and avoid using roads whenever possible. Using roads on the war front would likely result in an enemy attack. Government reports indicate that damage to fields, fences, and animals in the middle Tennessee area exceeded $4.5 million by the end of the war games. (CFF.)

Allied and Axis forces used more than 45 types of machine guns in World War II. Of the six or so different models used by US troops, the most common machine gun was the Browning M1917. One to three men could fire this heavy machine gun. If there were three men, one would direct the fire of the weapon, a second would fire it, and the third would feed the .30-caliber ammunition. This water-cooled model could fire 450–600 rounds per minute. The water helped keep the barrel cool so it would not explode or warp. Although it weighed less than 50 pounds, it was cumbersome to move because it also required the transport of water and a tripod. (Both, CFF.)

This photograph shows a typical machine gun nest with netting over it to help camouflage the men and the gun. Dry grass and branches were also used for concealment. The war games were designed to simulate the "reality" of war; however, live ammunition was generally used only on designated practice ranges. (NARA-CP.)

The 155-millimeter howitzer was a medium-size, long-range artillery weapon that weighed approximately 12,500 pounds and was towed by another vehicle. It had a range of 7,100 to 16,355 yards (four to nine miles) depending on the type of round fired. There were four types of shells available for this weapon: high explosive, chemical, illumination, and smoke. (CFF.)

Soldiers from Battery B demonstrated the 155-millimeter howitzer and the use of camouflage nets to visitors during Family Day on April 20, 1941. The howitzer was used in World War I, but numerous improvements were made to the weapon and carriage before it was adopted for use in World War II. The other fighting nations had similar medium artillery weapons on the battlefield. Firing the howitzer required a highly coordinated gunnery unit, as numerous steps had to be taken to ready the weapon: preparing the shell, cleaning the powder chamber, loading the shell, and aiming for the target. Additional communication and logistics soldiers were also part of a single howitzer battalion. (Both, MNA.)

The 240-millimeter howitzer was a super-heavy field artillery weapon. It weighed approximately 21 tons and had to be moved in sections. At least 14 men were needed to operate this weapon, plus hundreds of other soldiers to ready the projectiles, bring ammunition supplies to the site, operate communication lines, and perform other logistics for the unit. (CFF.)

Sgt. Leo Britt of Chattanooga, Tennessee, explains how a range finder works to his mother, L.J. Britt (left), and his fiancée, Louise Harris (right). The range finder operator aligned several prisms within the device to determine the distance to a particular object. This range finder is similar to modern-day survey equipment. (MNA.)

Sgt. John Kirnbauser (left) and Sgt. Fred Niebuhr (right) of the 108th Ordnance Company, 33rd Infantry Division, are using a special mounted rifle for training and practice. Ordnance companies were responsible for weapon and ammunition logistical support for both ground and air combat troops. The divisions eventually became responsible for attaining and maintaining vehicles. (NARA-CP.)

A young boy crouches near an artillery shell while visiting the base on family day. The artillery shell for the 155-millimeter howitzer weighed 95 pounds and could devastate an area approximately nine miles away and 50 yards wide. The 240-millimeter howitzer fired a 360-pound shell up to 25,225 yards (14 miles) and could easily annihilate concrete structures. (MNA.)

The military recognized the need for a vehicle that could keep up with the demands of the diverse terrains and climates that troops encountered. A standardized model eventually emerged from three prototype submissions, and from this, the military jeep was born. Given the overall size of the base, a jeep was the most efficient means of transportation. (NARA-CP.)

The walkie-talkie enabled air-to-land communication, allowing troops to easily send and receive reports on the movement of enemy forces. Soldiers were now mobile, which eliminated the need for individuals to physically deliver messages, as was the standard operating procedure in prior engagements. In the image at left, Pfc. James Prader reports the effects of artillery fire to a fire-control station. (NARA-CP.)

The Signal Corps was created in 1860, but in World War II, its size increased exponentially. The Signal Corps was responsible, in part, for military communication, intelligence, photography, and training throughout the world for ground, air, and sea divisions. This division fulfilled a vital communicative role ranging from the use of telephone and radar to Teletype and radio. (CFF.)

Over 650,000 jeeps were produced for the military from 1940 to 1945. These all-terrain vehicles were modified as needed by troops in the field. Radio communication units, as seen here, were installed in the back of jeeps to assist with field communications so that messages could be swiftly sent to advancing platoons. (NARA-CP.)

The deuce and a half (aka 2.5-ton 6x6) was one of the heavy-duty mechanized trucks used throughout the war to haul supplies and passengers. Later versions of the vehicle had a machine gun mount that enabled operators to quickly defend themselves if necessary. It was available in a multitude of configurations and specialty versions. (MNA.)

Soldiers simulate an attack on a light tank by throwing Molotov cocktails and sticky grenades from foxhole positions. The Molotov cocktail is a bottle-based incendiary device made from a flammable liquid with a cloth wick. The sticky grenade is another type of incendiary device that is manually placed or thrown within close proximity to a tank; its outer sticky substance is meant to adhere to the tank before detonating. (NARA-CP.)

Four

TRAINING FOR WAR

TECHNIQUES FOR SURVIVAL

From left to right, instructor Pvt. Louis D. Gerger of Company L, 131st Infantry Regiment, points out the location of Pearl Harbor on the globe to Pfc. Linn A. Holmes of Springfield, Illinois, and Sgt. Richard Coepke of Chicago, Illinois; the man at far right is unidentified. Geography lessons helped soldiers understand both where they would soon be deployed and how to follow the movement of enemy troops. (NARA-CP.)

The commissioned and noncommissioned officers of the 33rd Division watch Lt. Col. J.H. Harper of Waukegan, Illinois, and Sgt. Frederick Trevalio (holding projectile) demonstrate a Livens Projector during training at the Division Gas School. The Livens Projector, a motor-propelled device, had a range of 1,600 yards (roughly one mile) and was used to disburse chemicals and gases over the enemy. (NARA-CP.)

Military expertise was learned in and out of the classroom. Extensive classroom training ensured excellent mental aptitude in addition to top physical performance. Classes included topics on world trade and economics, theory and method of bridge design and construction, history, geography, current events, and military intelligence and organization. (NARA-CP.)

Gen. Ben Lear was intent on ensuring his men were a disciplined, professional army. This philosophy was evident after several soldiers engaged in lewd language and behavior toward several women on an Alabama golf course in the summer of 1941. When the soldiers failed to fall back in line upon General Lear's orders, the entire division was punished with a 15-mile hike in the blistering Alabama heat. Men under General Lear's command were expected to be disciplined gentlemen at all times. Above, Capt. Brook Wilson, commanding officer of the 80th Ron Troop, 80th Division, instructs a new cadre of men. At right, Sgt. Fred Peterson of Illinois lectures about the western hemisphere to members of Company A and Headquarters and Service Company of the 108th Engineer Battalion. (Both, NARA-CP.)

Gen. Ben Lear's training program deviated from traditional programs, as he was intent on providing soldiers with training that was as close to reality as possible. Here, Sgt. J.M. Compton (left) and 2nd Lt. W.E. Vazzana demonstrate how to tie down an opponent using only a rifle with a fixed bayonet. (NARA-CP.)

Improvements to the training program continually occurred based on information provided by combat reports and individuals returning from the war front. Here, Sgt. J.M. Compton (left) and 2nd Lt. W.E. Vazzana demonstrate how to attack an opponent from the rear to force him to the ground. (NARA-CP.)

Sgt. J.M. Compton (top) and 2nd Lt. W.E. Vazzana demonstrate a method of hand-to-hand combat to disarm an opponent with a fixed bayonet from the rear. Once a fight was on the ground, dirty fighting tactics could be used. Dirty fighting taught men to use every possible advantage during combat. The notions of a "clean and honest" fight were no longer applicable when exchanging blows with enemies. (NARA-CP.)

Sgt. J.M. Compton (left) and 2nd Lt. W.E. Vazzana demonstrate position No. 4 from the Rangers Manual for hand-to-hand combat. With this method, the goal is to twist the opponent's left hand with a downward thrust. This move will make the opponent release his hold on his rifle. (NARA-CP.)

Swim trials helped discern each soldier's overall strength and ability as a swimmer. Although numerous men drowned during practice, these exercises prepared soldiers for situations when they might have to swim across a river because a bridge had been blown up or carry a pioneer towline so a rope bridge could then be erected to allow remaining soldiers to cross. (Susan Wesley.)

Soldiers were classified into one of four types of swimmers: beginner (C) test, intermediate (B) test, advanced (A) test, and expert (AA) test. The War Department outlined water-related best practices in the Watermanship Basic Field Manual (FM 21–22). The manual covered topics such as swimming, floating survival at sea, and how to abandon a sinking ship. At left are two unidentified soldiers participating in swim trials. (Susan Wesley.)

The Watermanship Basic Field Manual defined military swimming as a fully clothed and equipped soldier being able to reach his destination via water and arriving ready for action. Men were taught to conserve energy and ensure buoyancy until rescue arrived. In this water training class, men are being schooled in commando tactics under the supervision of the American Red Cross. (NARA-CP.)

Observation planes performed a variety of functions throughout the war—reconnaissance, ambulance, and cargo delivery. The types of planes used by American troops varied, but they were utilized by both ground and sea forces. Here, a plane from the 127th Observation Squadron is picking up a message. (NARA-CP.)

Recon Company of the 775th Tank Destroyer Battalion is shown practicing to prepare a jeep to float across Cumberland Springs. The jeep was carefully centered on a large piece of canvas, which was then tightly fastened around it to make it watertight. Any excess water inside the canvas was pumped out, and the jeep was launched into the water. The soldiers swam the vehicle to the other side of the river and removed the canvas. The vehicle was then driven out of the water and onto dry land. Understanding how to successfully transport equipment and vehicles over bodies of water saved valuable time, as building any type of bridge could take considerable time and manpower. (Both, NARA-CP.)

Heavier equipment and vehicles were transported across bodies of water and down rivers using pontoon floats. Pontoons had been used for centuries to create bridges because of their sturdy construction. These soldiers are moving a 1.5-ton Chevrolet truck across Cumberland Springs using a pneumatic pontoon. (NARA-CP.)

Combat training was brutal but necessary. Here, Sgt. Edward Arendt of Illinois faces his "enemy attacker" with grim determination. A rifle generally came with two accessories: a bayonet and a grenade launcher. The bayonet is a long knife attached to the end of the rifle, and the grenade launcher could fire antitank and antipersonnel grenades. (NARA-CP.)

In this stream-crossing demonstration, men from the 775th D Battalion use an improvised raft to cross Cumberland Lake. In addition to knowing how to swim and construct rafts, soldiers had to learn basic water navigation principles to ensure they would arrive at the appropriate destination. Men would use charts, a compass, a watch, and either the sun or stars for navigation. (NARA-CP.)

These men—Sgt. J.M. Compton (left) and 2nd Lt. W.E. Vazzara—use combat training skills and a rifle to wrestle the enemy to the ground. Wrestling an opponent to the ground required speed and agility. The military had five principles a solider followed to ground the enemy: use your stomach, maintain balance, maintain momentum, inflict pain, and use deception to your advantage. (NARA-CP.)

Sgt. Milo Mideleton demonstrates how to disarm a rifleman (in this case, Sgt. Edward Arendt). Both men were from Illinois and members of the 129th Infantry Regiment. Once the enemy and his rifle had been separated, the man could be thrown to the ground. Effective throwing moves required the soldier to use his hips, shoulders, wrist, and back to ground the opponent. (NARA-CP.)

Men of the 130th Infantry Regiment practice traversing a ditch using a rope swing on the obstacle course. The rope swing was part of the physical fitness obstacle course. The climbing, jumping, swinging, and crawling activities found throughout the course were designed to increase a soldier's physical and mental stamina. (NARA-CP.)

Gen. Ben Lear stressed physical fitness and conditioning in addition to classroom learning. For a soldier, being able to think on one's feet was vital to survival. Here, men from Company D of 129th Infantry—Pfc. Uge Ozzi, Pvt. Anthony Ferrara, Cpl. Floyd Fitzpatrick, and Pvt. Carl Kruman—play a game of "horse and rider." (NARA-CP.)

Sgt. J.M. Compton (top) and 2nd Lt. W.E. Vazzana demonstrate a method of dirty fighting tactics. Soldiers were instructed to use their bodies as weapons when necessary. By using one's head, teeth, elbows, hands, fists, knees, and/or feet, a soldier could disable or kill an assailant. (NARA-CP.)

A panel truck was transformed into the 33rd Division's radio communication vehicle, which was outfitted with the latest equipment. From this mobile unit, soldiers like Private Pecker were able to maintain consistent communication with troops on the front lines to provide appropriate orders. (NARA-CP.)

A quarter-ton truck floats across a stream after being wrapped in a 2.5-ton truck cover in preparation for moving across the river. Soldiers utilized different elements of their training to move large vehicles across a river, judging the depth of a river and the swiftness of its currents, buoyancy of the vehicle, physical fitness, and ability of the vehicle to move across the opposite bank. (NARA-CP.)

The model Nazi village was built as part of the Ranger Training Program. It provided Rangers with street-to-street combat to attain experience for situations that would likely be encountered in cities overseas. The real-life scenarios helped reduce soldiers' fear and anticipation levels, sharpen mental keenness, and build muscle memory. The village was replete with German signage and a caricature of the Führer. Mock villages were also constructed at several other US military bases. In Utah, German and Japanese villages were painstakingly re-created based on those in each county and had representative furnishings to enable the military to test the precision of its bombs. The villages were rebuilt after each bombing to allow for continuous training. (Both, NARA-CP.)

Above, S.Sgt. Bishop Scarboro (left), Cpl. Elmer Cochran (center, top), and Sgt. Edward Draper demonstrate a method of entering and covering a building while "mopping up" the enemy village, which referred to the final clearing of any remaining enemy combatants in a given area. These operations were not necessarily quick and easy; each one varied significantly. Some combatants would continue to wage war in the hope that reinforcements would soon arrive. Other times, those that remained willingly surrendered. Below, Sergeant Draper, Sgt. J. Perna, and Pvt. Russell Scarboro simulate an attack on the city hall of the model Nazi village. In the training exercise, live ammunition was used to fire at dummy targets or above soldiers' heads. (Both, NARA-CP.)

A soldier attacks the "enemy" with his bayonet at one of the buildings in the model Nazi village. Note Hitler's image in the window. In a real-life situation, the World War II soldier's end goal would be to kill the assailant. If the bayonet attack did not kill the opponent, dirty fighting would most likely ensue given the close proximity of the men. (NARA-CP.)

Soldiers of the 129th Infantry Regiment maneuver through barbed wire to learn how to avoid injury and traverse such entanglements in a short period of time. Germans used barbed wire in their lines of defense, installing it along cliffs, beaches, roads, and fences. Any area that needed fortifying typically had some type of barbed wire strung on or around it. (NARA-CP.)

Soldiers had to carefully watch where they walked and what they touched, as a booby trap could be hidden anywhere. Toward the end of the war, Germans became notorious for planting booby traps everywhere—from a bar of chocolate and a mess kit to a vase of flowers and a chair. At right, Sgt. H.H. Spencer removes a picture on the wall to reveal a booby trap that has a one-pound charge of dynamite attached to it. The booby trap below ignites a two-pound charge of dynamite when the bottle of Scotch is picked up. These methods were just a few of the ways that American soldiers learned how to both set their own booby traps and avoid those set by others. (Both, NARA-CP.)

Two Ranger students practice hand-to-hand combat and learn to disarm an opponent who is armed with a knife. Once disarmed, the enemy could be assaulted in sensitive areas of the body, such as the temples, bridge of the nose, base of the skull, upper jaw, or kidneys. (NARA-CP.)

The obstacle course simulated many of the potential conditions a solider might encounter on the front lines. Here, Pvt. Nicolas Gomez and Pfc. Mike Danatako demonstrate how to descend a cliff using ropes. Knowing how to scale a cliff was a useful skill, as such obstacles were prevalent in the European theater. (NARA-CP.)

Infantry soldiers trained to overcome any type of impediment. These men are jumping from one of the 10-foot-high fences on the obstacle course. Knowing how to land without breaking a foot or twisting an ankle was critical to survival; an injured man who did not have a gaping wound might not receive immediate medical attention during the heat of battle. (NARA-CP.)

Soldiers inspect damage caused by bazooka antitank rocket launchers fired at the US Second Army Ranger School. This was a small arms weapon that one or two men could discharge by holding it over the shoulder. Soldiers dubbed it the Buck Rogers rocket gun after the popular comic strip *Buck Rogers in the 25th Century A.D.* (NARA-CP.)

US troops had access to numerous small arms: rifles, pistols, and machine guns. Depending on the model, a rifle could have a range of 600 to 1,320 feet. The pistol's range was 82 feet, and the tommy gun's range was 656 feet. Sgt. A. Colasanti (left), Cpl. M. Riesenberg (center), and Cpl. B. Blake fire a rifle, tommy gun, and pistol, respectively. (NARA-CP.)

Given its size, the parade field could also be used as a landing strip. Sometimes small passenger and observation planes took off and landed using this area at the base rather than William Northern Field. Generally, the passenger planes that used the parade field as a landing strip carried high-ranking military personnel or dignitaries. (NARA-CP.)

Five

Tennessee Maneuvers
Practicing for War

Soldiers were trained to solve numerous tactical problems during simulated battle conditions. Here, a corporal of the 33rd Reconnaissance Company advances through a smoke screen. Gen. Ben Lear felt that exposing men to realistic battlefield scenarios while training would empower them to act decisively in their first encounters with the enemy in the theater of war, which would hopefully bring more men home safely. (NARA-CP.)

Full armored divisions participated in the war game maneuvers, thus crops were often destroyed. An armored division typically consisted of tank battalions, personnel carriers, ambulances, supply vehicles, signal corps, engineering support units, and other military vehicles. The federal government generally reimbursed farmers for the damages to their fields. (Susan Wesley.)

Another centuries-old technology used by the military in World War II was the aerial ropeway. This was apt for moving vehicles, supplies, and people in areas where the terrain consisted of deep valleys and small gorges or if a bridge had been destroyed. These Rangers are learning how to ferry a jeep across a river using overhead cables. (NARA-CP.)

Men of the Army Ranger School are shown crossing a toggle rope bridge while taking fire from live rounds of machine guns, rifles, hand grenades, small dynamite land mines, and mortars. Live ammunition was not generally used in training, but as troops neared the end of their training, it was important for them to be exposed to the sights, sounds, and smells that were indicative of real combat. Being able to overcome the initial shock and stress that resulted from these types of situations helped men become better battlefield tacticians when the threat of death was a constant reality. (Both, NARA-CP.)

War games enacted specific battle plans during each 8- to 12-week simulation. Unfortunately, these simulations were not without causalities. Approximately 268 deaths occurred in Tennessee due to the maneuvers. War games were also conducted in Louisiana and California. In this photograph, a convoy on maneuver stops and awaits further instruction. (Susan Wesley.)

Less than 80 years prior to the Tennessee Maneuvers, numerous Civil War battles were fought on the same lands in the cities of Tullahoma, Murfreesboro, Nashville, and Chattanooga. Gen. Braxton Bragg set up the Army of Tennessee headquarters in the Tullahoma area after the Battle of Murfreesboro. Control of the area was finally relinquished through the Tullahoma campaign of Gen. Williams S. Rosecrans. This image shows a Camp Forrest convoy in the middle distance. (CFF.)

This view overlooks one of the many valleys in Middle Tennessee, which is an area that spans close to 41 square miles. The area around Camp Forrest was approximately 1,070 feet above sea level and only 15 miles from the mountains. The Middle Tennessee area spans approximately 41 counties and has 12 different lakes. (CFF.)

The lack of adequate barracks required numerous troops to live in tents, especially during the maneuvers. These conditions continually presented health and sanitary problems for the men due to the lack of latrine and bathing facilities. However, it exposed them to the harsh realities they would soon face and taught them how best to overcome potential health-related issues. (Susan Wesley.)

Bathing on maneuvers was generally accomplished via a makeshift field shower using a 36-gallon Lister bag similar to the one seen here. The lack of adequate shower facilities was problematic, as appropriate health and sanitation measures were overlooked. Sometimes, local residents would rent out their tub and shower facilities for a nominal fee. There were also several hospitality centers that allowed soldiers to use their facilities. (CFF.)

There were no laundry services available on maneuvers, but sometimes local families would wash clothes for the men. When kind strangers were unavailable, men had to wash their clothes and hang them to dry on a line. Washing clothes during maneuvers generally did not occur often; it was done only when it was convenient. Delousing powder was sometimes used when bathing was not practical. (CFF.)

Soldiers on maneuvers generally had food items like sugar and coffee that were rationed or unavailable to civilians. Governmental regulations stipulated that unused provisions must be buried before moving on to the next camp. However, to repay the local families for their hospitality and kindness, soldiers would give them these commodities rather than waste them. This photograph depicts chow time while on maneuvers. (CFF.)

The Sanitation Field Manual indicates that troops on maneuvers should bury refuse in pits away from the bivouac area, then cover them with mounded dirt each day to eliminate odors and flies and deter wild animals. Following appropriate sanitation protocols ensured each soldier remained healthy. These soldiers are preparing a garbage pit while on maneuvers. (CFF.)

The US Army Corps of Engineers regiments were responsible for a multitude of combat support functions for both ground and aerial troops. Each regiment's support functions were all-encompassing and might include activities like general construction, bridge construction and maintenance, vehicle maintenance, mapping, and securing water supplies. By keeping the units moving forward, these divisions helped thwart advancing enemies. On the home front, these divisions were tasked with helping repair damages to local farms and communities caused by the "red and blue armies" (the names given to the two sides in war games) during maneuvers. Thanks to this practice, the corps could quickly and efficiently ready the necessary infrastructure for combat and infantry divisions once overseas. In these photographs, the 305th Engineering Battalion practices blowing up a bridge over the Little Tennessee River. (Both, TSLA.)

This photograph shows the remnants of the bridge on the opposite page after it was destroyed. Bridges were continually built and blown up throughout the Middle Tennessee area. These exercises allowed the US Army Corps of Engineer divisions to practice before attempting to undertake such measures in the European theater. (TSLA.)

Major General Richardson, commanding general, and 2nd Lt. P.F. Carney, general's aide, are two of the men shown here walking across the Elk River via a footbridge. The Elk River, which is 195 miles long, runs through the Middle Tennessee area. Camp Forrest's water supply was pumped from this river, and it currently supplies water to the base's successor, Arnold Air Force Base. (NARA-CP.)

The Spencer Artillery Range was completed in 1941. Located on more than 30,000 acres, it was used as an impact area for bombers and a practice area for large artillery weapons as well as smaller handheld weapons such as pistols, rifles, and machine guns. The site had several observational towers and ammunition storage buildings. Today, residents are told to use caution when exploring these areas, as unexploded ordnance still pose a potential hazard. (CFF.)

The artillery range was approximately 40 miles from the main cantonment. The Second Air Force also used it as a bomb range. Bombers used large sacks of grain and flour to simulate bombs rather than firing live rounds. Ranges were also available to hone shooting skills with smaller arms. (CFF.)

In these field exercises, the machine gun crew of Recon Company, 775 Tank Destroyer Battalion, is holding its position from the approaching enemy. With these types of tactical problems, soldiers learned how to quickly stop advancing enemy convoys. This proficiency was just one of the many enemy combat tactics taught in the various training courses. (NARA-CP.)

During the World War II era, barbed wire was the prevailing material used to keep animals in their pastures. In this photograph, instructors on the wire entanglements course demonstrate how to cut barbed wire using a cloth wrapped around pliers in an effort to muffle the sound. Soldiers could potentially move undetected by muffling this noise. (NARA-CP.)

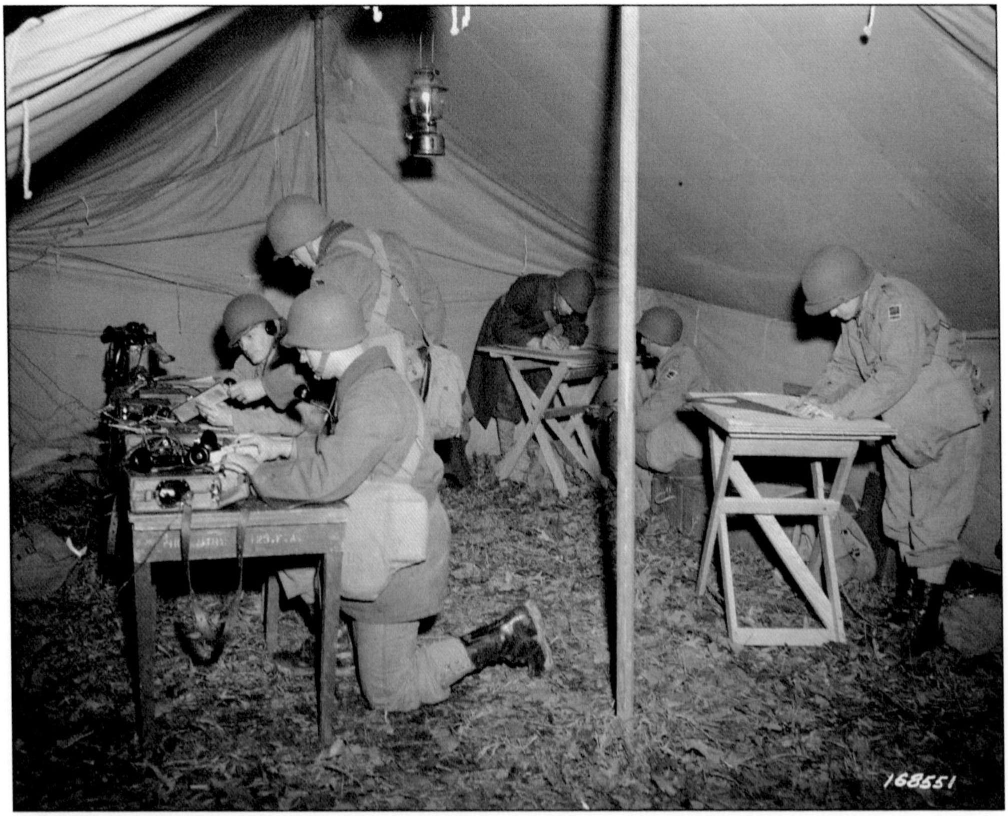

Maneuvers simulated live action that soldiers would soon face on the war front. Pictured working from a field command center are, in no particular order, Cpl. T.G. Mason, "B" Battery; Pfc. A.F. Stauffer, "A" Battery; Pvt. G.S. Woreley, Headquarters Battery; T/5 J.T. Meachae, HCO Headquarters Battery; Capt. H.M. Marx, Battalion S-3; and Pfc. Glenn Robins, VCO Headquarters Battery. (NARA-CP.)

To appropriately replicate the conditions of a loaded plane, units were instructed to fill planes with large sacks of flour and cornmeal in lieu of actual bombs. These measures allowed pilots to understand differences in takeoff speeds and flight maneuvers necessary for loaded versus unloaded planes. This is one of the observation planes used for training at Camp Forrest and William Northern Field. (CFF.)

History is replete with the use of chemical weapons in warfare. Although some generations frowned upon using them, advancements in their overall effectiveness continued throughout World War II. Some of the more common gases used were mustard gas and phosgene. Knowing when and how to properly wear a gas mask was a vital part of basic military training. Failure to understand these basic principles could have fatal consequences. (CFF.)

Communication lines were strung using poles or trees. The latter provided a much quicker and cheaper way to set up a communication command post (as opposed to transporting poles and digging holes). Here, a soldier is preparing to attach communication lines to a tree. (Susan Wesley.)

Tullahoma residents and military leaders worked to ensure that socially acceptable forms of entertainment were continually available for soldiers. While on maneuvers, a mobile USO unit would visit troops to bring them movies, music, newspapers, magazines, and mail. In this photograph, a soldier clowns around for the camera during downtime on the Tennessee Maneuvers. (CFF.)

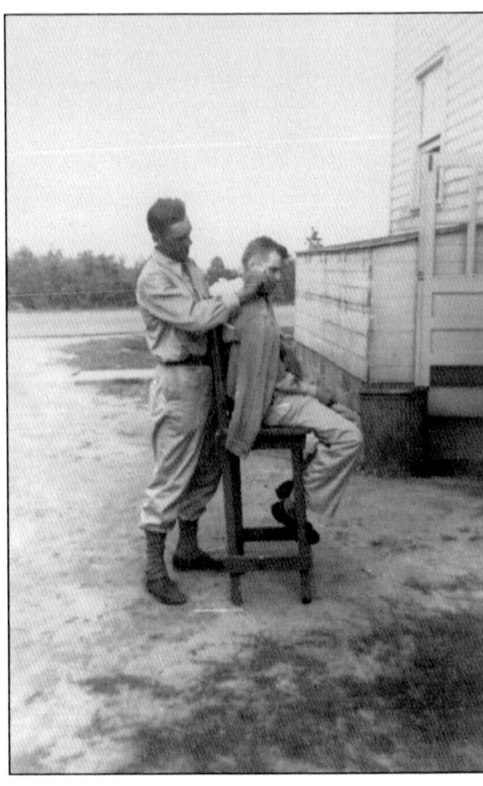

Personal appearance was a very important aspect of military life. Men were expected to be clean-shaven and maintain an appropriate military haircut; however, this was not always feasible during combat. Whenever possible, soldiers on the march could fill their helmets with water to shave and bathe. Personal hygiene was not only important for appearance but also for health and sanitation. (CFF.)

A solider poses for the camera while standing in one of the many streams encountered during maneuvers. (CFF.)

Soldiers on the battlefield had to carry all of their possessions with them. Their packs typically weighed over 60 pounds and contained a blanket, tent, overshoes, mess kit, knife, fork, spoon, bayonet, scabbard, cartridge belt, first-aid kit, knapsack, raincoat, tent spikes, rifle, and canteen. (Susan Wesley.)

Convoys became a typical sight during the war era, as they were used to transport supplies and troops throughout the Middle Tennessee area. Roads became extremely congested due to the increased presence of military vehicles. The government constructed roads specifically designed for military use to several cities within a 30-mile radius to help minimize traffic jams. (CFF.)

Protecting soldiers from illness or disease due to food contamination was one of the military's primary concerns. The Sanitation Field Manual detailed proper methods for how encampments should store and cook food, as well as how to clean and disinfect cooking and eating utensils. This is a typical cook tent erected during maneuvers. (CFF.)

Six

Visitation and Celebration

Downtime While Waiting for War

Visiting dignitaries were often treated to a review of the troops and a demonstration of some of the large military weapons, such as the 155-millimeter howitzer. Some notable dignitaries who visited Camp Forrest included ranking diplomats, naval and military officers of 13 Latin American countries, and Pres. Franklin D. Roosevelt. Pictured is President Roosevelt's review of the troops and some of the modern weapons of war. (Franklin Roosevelt Presidential Library.)

On the afternoon of Saturday, April 17, 1943, Pres. Franklin D. Roosevelt stopped at Camp Forrest as part of his second wartime tour of military posts, naval stations, and war factories. As shown below, Gov. Prentice Cooper (in the driver's-side rear seat), Lt. Gen. Ben Lear (in the passenger-side rear seat), and Maj. Gen. Horace L. McBride (driver's seat) accompanied the president (passenger seat) on his inspection of the facility and troops. During the brief visit, honor detachments from the 318th and 319th Infantry Bands played, and a gun salute of 35-millimeter howitzers was fired by the 314th Field Artillery. The men of the 80th Division and various Second Army troops lined the roads for inspection. Presidential reports note the troops appeared to be comprised of seasoned men who were ready for duty anywhere. (Both, Franklin Roosevelt Presidential Library.)

Franklin D. Roosevelt's 1940 presidential election was a landslide victory. This election cemented his third term as the nation's commander in chief. In addition to overcoming the devastating efforts of both the Great Depression and a world war, his 12 years as president (1933–1945) brought about significant national changes. President Roosevelt passed away from a stroke just months into his fourth term and only a month before the war in Europe ended. Above, President Roosevelt thanks one of Camp Forrest's commanding officers for his service and dedication to the war effort. At right, the president shakes Tennessee governor Prentice Cooper's hand. (Both, Franklin Roosevelt Presidential Library.)

Parting is such sweet sorrow was often all too true, as friends and family members continually worried whether their men-at-arms would safely return. Unfortunately, many of them would never come home. Although estimates vary, reports indicate that over 70 million people perished in World War II. (CFF.)

Enjoying a gathering at Camp Forrest are, from left to right, Maj. W. Wimble (post special services officer), Col. M.F. Waltz (camp commander), Gov. Prentice Cooper, Sgt. Alvin York, and Brig. Gen. Frank Mahin (33rd Division commander). Sergeant York was a decorated World War I hero who sought to increase educational opportunities upon his return home. (NARA-CP.)

Mother's Day ceremonies were held at the service club in May 1942. Mothers arrived by special bus from Illinois and other states to attend the gala celebration. Events included a coast-to-coast broadcast on CBS. Virginia Covington of College Grove, Tennessee, was chosen as "Dear Mom" of Camp Forrest from among the more than 1,000 Tennessee mothers who sought the honor. (NARA-CP.)

A large reception was held in Virginia Covington's honor, and she was greeted by hundreds of soldiers and visitors. She was presented with a $1,000 war bond by post commander Col. M.F. Waltz. Her son, Maj. William L. Covington, who was stationed at Fort Custer, made a special trip to Camp Forrest for the ceremony. (NARA-CP.)

The post exchange (PX) afforded soldiers the opportunity to purchase items such as toiletries, cigarettes, candy, and postcards. At Camp Forrest, civilians generally staffed the PXs. Here, Pvt. Robert Cooke (left) of Chattanooga, Tennessee, and Pvt. Charles Britton of Michigan are assisted by clerks Clara Hill and Margie Green, both of Chattanooga, Tennessee, at one of the base's PXs. (MNA.)

Understanding the need for a place where soldiers could purchase "comfort items" while on base, the military formally created the PX at the onset of World War II. There were 58 PXs on base, with separate stores for officers versus enlisted men. This photograph shows the interior of a typical PX. (CFF.)

Since most entertainments in town were overcrowded, additional events like boxing matches were scheduled at the base's sports arena. In this match, Pvt. F. Guerra (left) fights A. Kophart, who was the featherweight champion of Alabama. Guerra won the fight by a decision. (NARA-CP.)

The *Chattanooga Times* newspaper and golfers from Chattanooga donated equipment for the nine-hole golf course at Camp Forrest. Austin White (second from right), of the *Chattanooga Times*, is congratulated by Capt. R.H. Zehm (second from left), of the camp athletic office, for the donation while Chesher Holmes (far left) and Capt. Benjamin Gause (far right) look on. Former professionals offered expert instruction to help soldiers improve their game. (NARA-CP.)

In addition to events at the base's sports arena, there were numerous recreational activities available to soldiers. For those who preferred quieter activities, there was a library stocked with newspapers, magazines, and books. In this photograph, James R. "Jim" Campbell enjoys a game of badminton. (Susan Wesley.)

Although living quarters were separated by race and gender, men and women were free to socialize with one another during the day. (CFF.)

Big bands toured large and small towns and military installations throughout the United States during World War II. The sounds of swing and jazz filled the air as a perfect momentary distraction from the war. Popular bands of the day included those of Glenn Miller, Artie Shaw, and Duke Ellington. Here, Bobby Byrne and his orchestra entertain soldiers at the Camp Forrest Service Club. (NARA-CP.)

Music helped lift the spirits of Americans at home and at war. As radios became more accessible, so did the tunes from popular composers like Irving Berlin and Johnny Mercer and vocalists Ella Fitzgerald, Bing Crosby, and the Andrews Sisters. Several men from a military band are shown here entertaining fellow soldiers. (CFF.)

The Clarksville Business and Professional Women's Club furnished the dayroom for the men of Battery G. From left to right are Jessie Mae Collier, Bessie Collier, Capt. Murray Johnson (commanding officer of Battery G of 181st), Mrs. Johnson, Lt. James Hollums, Edna Uffelman, Lt. C.B. Martin, Mrs. Martin, and Mrs. Fred Davidson Sr. (MNA.)

From far and wide, Americans supported the war effort. This was shown in the development of numerous women's clubs that sprang up across the nation as women united to gather basic necessities for the servicemen. In Chicago, the "Roll out the Barrel" drive collected over 20 barrels filled with gum, cigarettes, records, and sports equipment for the "boys" at Camp Forrest. In this image, Tullahoma residents are supporting one of the many military bands. (MNA.)

There were 12 chapels located throughout the base and four permanently stationed chaplains. Regular worship services were available for Catholic, Jewish, and Protestant faiths. Chapels had organs that could be easily interchanged to correspond to each type of service. Chaplains Fielder (left) and Cash are shown presiding over a service at one of the camp's chapels. (NARA-CP.)

Here, members of an African American battalion choir sing at one of the camp's chapels. Segregation was the norm in the South—even during the war. The federal government enacted several laws regarding discrimination, but they did not affect the prevailing mindset. Camp Forrest was segregated, but very little documentation is available regarding the amenities for African American troops. Amid discrimination at home, these men and women fought bravely throughout the war. (NARA-CP.)

The war's impact on Hollywood was apparent in the films that were released during that time. These movies were not just entertainment for the masses—they also helped maintain military and civilian morale. Popular war movies of the day included *Thirty Seconds Over Tokyo, The Battle of Midway*, and *They Were Expendable*. Each night, at least one of the four movie theaters on base hosted a screening. Hollywood also helped produce military training films, which covered various topics on warfare and weapons. Above is the exterior of a Camp Forrest movie theater, and below is the interior of another. (Above, CFF; below, MNA.)

Camp Forrest had two service clubs with cafeterias and soda fountains. In addition to weekly dances, the base service clubs hosted activities such as entertainment from noted Hollywood personalities, remote radio broadcasts, and the 1942 Mother's Day celebration. The USO worked with the base service club director to coordinate other socially acceptable forms of entertainment that would keep morale and patriotism levels high. (CFF.)

The officer and service club cafeterias allowed soldiers and their guests to dine on base at reasonable prices. A menu from Camp Forrest detailed available entrees: hamburgers (15¢), cheeseburgers (20¢), BLTs (20¢), various other sandwiches (15–25¢), steak ($2) and chicken ($1.50) dinners, soups (varied prices), and vegetables (varied prices). (NARA-CP.)

These soldiers served their county for decades before arriving at Camp Forrest: 1st Sgt. Homer P. Lott (left) of Philadelphia, Pennsylvania, had 26 years of service; S.Sgt. Mack S. Davis (center) of Altoona, Alabama, had 30 years of service; and Sgt. Weaver A. Briscoe of Philadelphia, Pennsylvania, had 20 years of service. All of these men also served at Camp Forrest. (NARA-CP.)

Troops proudly display the colors while the military band plays during a parade through town on family day. Members of the military band served as both soldiers and musicians. These men participated in basic training exercises, mastered specific military band formation and movement drills, and practiced with bandmates. (MNA.)

Women served in a variety of noncombat military roles in World War II. The women's military service branches included the following: Women Air Force Service Pilots (WASPs), Women's Army Corps (WAC), Navy Women's Reserve (WAVES), Marine Corps Women's Reserve, Coast Guard Women's Reserve (SPARS), Army Nurse Corps, and Navy Nurse Corps. Gen. Dwight D. Eisenhower remarked on the value of women's service to the war effort, whether on a farm, in a factory, or in a uniform. Above, members of the Army Nurse Corps participate in a family day parade. Below, members of a WAC detachment also march proudly in the parade. (Both, MNA.)

Troop mascots were common in World War II. These animals provided companionship, morale boosts, and stress release for the soldiers. Tales of heroic feats from canine companions at the front include alerting troops of approaching enemies or that chemical gas was wafting toward them. The first dog to receive a military designation was Sergeant Stubby in World War I. At left, troop mascot Brownie poses for the camera. Below, Big Boy Sarg, the mascot of the 75th Brigade Field Artillery, is accompanied by Pvt. W.D. MacDonald (left), Pvt. Howard Harrison (center), and Pvt. Dallas Roberts, all from Lebanon, Tennessee. (Left, CFF; below, MNA.)

Here, a Tennessee National Guard unit and their canine mascot disembark the train and march to their barracks. Dogs also served in World War II in the Dogs for Defense program. The military asked its citizenry to donate their pets to the war effort. Americans answered the call by sending over 40,000 dogs to help defeat the Axis powers. Many divisions reported that the program was a resounding success. (MNA.)

Lt. Col. James Sammis and musical comedy and radio starlet Joan Winters salute the colors at the 108th Quartermaster Battalion parade. During her visit, Winters was given the silver shoulder eagles of a colonel and the unit's official insignia. Among her many performances was the starring role on the radio soap opera *Girl Alone*. (NARA-CP.)

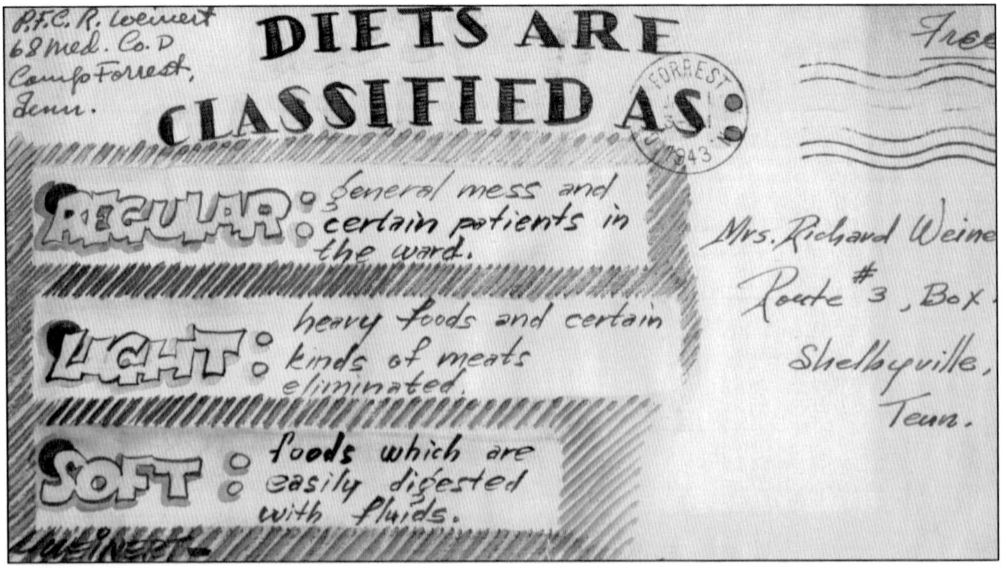

Although telephones were available throughout the post, it was not always easy to place a call or to reach one's desired party. When the base opened, the Tullahoma telephone services were antiquated and unable to meet the needs of the ever-increasing population. The problems were quickly ameliorated as dial service replaced crank phone systems and a new updated telephone station was constructed. Not all difficulties—such as attempting to place a call during peak times—were eliminated; however, the swift corrective response did allow homesick soldiers to hear the voices of their loved ones back home. Generally, most soldiers sent letters and postcards to family and friends. (Both, CFF.)

Soldiers' correspondence described daily events and activities occurring in their respective lives. Some soldiers decorated the outside of envelopes with drawings. Each of these drawings was done by medic Cpl. Richard Weinert of the 68th Medical Regiment, Company D, on mail he sent to his girlfriend, Evelyn York (she became his wife when they married in 1942). Although Shelbyville, Tennessee, was only a short distance away from Camp Forrest, the couple wrote to one another at least once or twice a week. After the war, the couple returned to Wisconsin, and Weinert worked as a commercial artist for several different publications. Weinert passed away in 2001, but his artwork still provides a colorful glimpse of when the world was at war. (Both, CFF.)

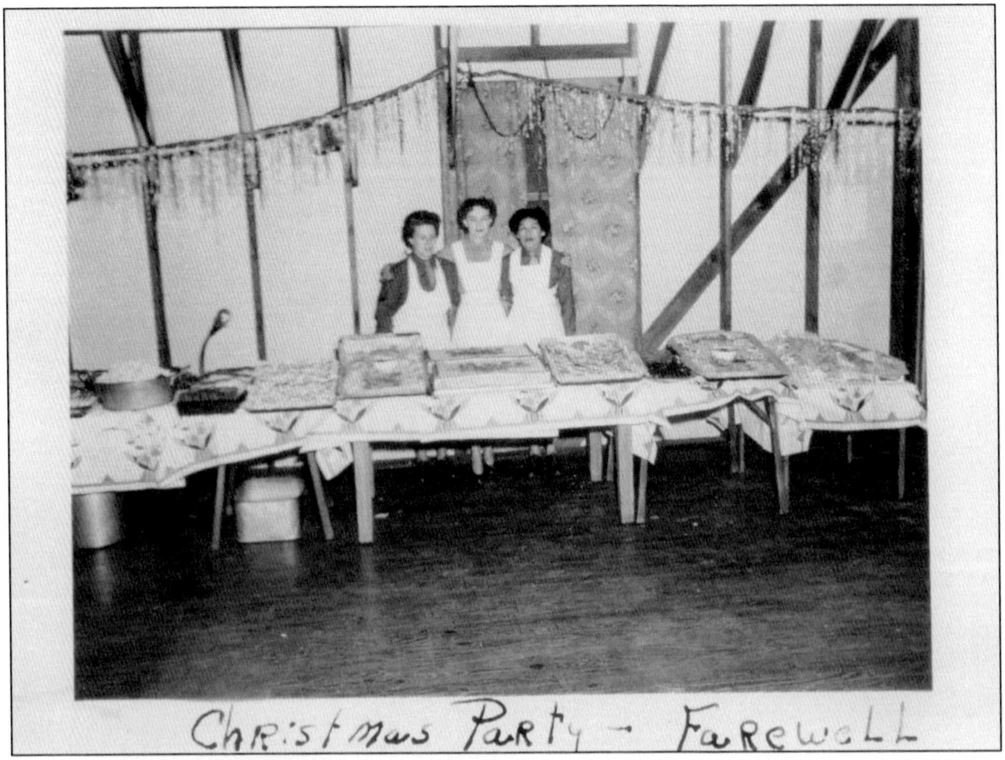

In 1943, the USO and women's groups hosted Christmas Eve and Christmas Day festivities to ensure the holidays were special for soldiers who were unable to be at home with family and friends. Articles in the *Putnam County Herald* newspaper reported that on Christmas Day, soldiers and guests were treated to "2,400 cups of coffee, 74 home baked cakes, 100 pounds of homemade candy, 5 bushels of apples, 6 crates of oranges, 300 packets of cigarettes, and 576 Hershey bars." Additionally, citizens donated wrapped presents so each soldier would have a gift to open on Christmas. (Both, USAWM.)

Chaplain Fielder (center), of the 4th Canadian Army Service Corps, chats with Sgt. and Mrs. Donald Lee after a service on base. Chaplain Fielder married the couple on base. Numerous marriages took place on and off base before soldiers were shipped off to war. Travelers Aid helped arrange over 300 marriages on base during the war years. (NARA-CP.)

There were a few guesthouses available on base that could accommodate visitors. Given the high demand for rooms, visitors were limited to a two-night stay. Those who wished to stay longer had to find alternate accommodations in Tullahoma, where there were a few boardinghouses and some rooms to rent from local residents. (Lisa Ramsey.)

Dayrooms provided a typical livable, homelike atmosphere where soldiers could relax when not in the classroom, at training, or on maneuvers. Funds used to decorate the 88 dayrooms at Camp Forrest were typically donated from local and national civic organizations and women's groups. (NARA-CP.)

In this photograph, soldiers of the 33rd Signal Company and their guests are indulging in cake and ice cream after a dance at the USO in Tullahoma. The USO provided soldiers with wholesome hospitality centers; these fell in line with Gen. Ben Lear's personal rules of conduct issued in 1943, which dictated that soldiers behave as gentlemen and only frequent military-approved establishments. (NARA-CP.)

Seven

TULLAHOMA
THE NEIGHBORING TOWN

The population of Tullahoma dramatically increased due to the establishment of Camp Forrest. In 1940, the population was 4,500; however, by the end of the war, the population had swelled to 75,000. Residents became accustomed to crowded stores, soldiers bivouacking in fields and on lawns, traffic jams, blackouts, and property destruction. (CFF.)

The United Service Organization (USO) evolved from Pres. Franklin D. Roosevelt's efforts to unite several civilian organizations into one that worked cohesively to support soldiers and their families. The organization arranged USO shows at home and abroad to boost morale. This is the USO club on Jackson Street; there were five USO clubs located throughout Tullahoma. (CFF.)

Numerous forms of transportation were available in the area. Train service was provided by the Nashville, Chattanooga & St. Louis Railroad. Soldiers could visit other cities, such as Nashville and Chattanooga, via the train. The train ride from Tullahoma to Nashville was about two and a half hours. There were also taxis, bus stations, and a civilian airport in Chattanooga and Nashville. Under Gen. Ben Lear's orders, soldiers were prohibited from hitchhiking. (CFF.)

There was a "classified" post office on base and a civilian post office in town. The number of postal workers at the civilian post office more than doubled throughout the war period. During peak periods, such as holidays, more than 150 postal workers were employed here to ensure mail was delivered on time. (CFF.)

Prior to the opening of the station hospital, soldiers were treated at Queen City Hospital. Venereal disease (VD) was one of the more prevalent medical issues for military personnel. Clinics throughout town and on base were set up to diagnose and treat this ailment. (CFF.)

In addition to the religious services and chapels on base, the town contained churches representing almost every denomination. These churches welcomed soldiers to attend services and participate in sponsored educational and recreational activities. Some of the churches included the First Baptist Church, St. Barnabas Episcopal Church, the Lutheran church, the M.E. church, and First Presbyterian Church. (CFF.)

Hotel King was one of the larger hotels in the area. Its large dining room in the Minors Restaurant was downsized to create a room of cots that could be rented nightly. Newspaper accounts at the time indicate that there were also seven restaurants, three drugstores, two five-and-ten stores, three men's and five women's clothing stores, and a movie theater in town. (CFF.)

Eight

POWs
The Aftermath of War

Camp Forrest became one of the nation's largest POW facilities starting in May 1942. More than 24,000 Italian and German POWs were held at the facility until the end of World War II. These men worked in a variety of positions at the station hospital, mess halls, and farms within the surrounding area. (TSLA.)

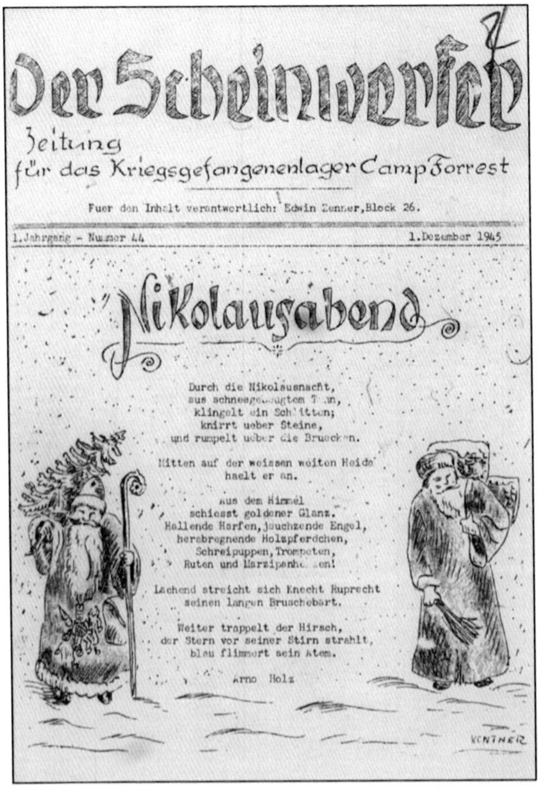

Der Scheinwerfer

Zeitung
für das Kriegsgefangenenlager Camp Forrest

Fuer den Inhalt verantwortlich: Edwin Zenner, Block 26.

1. Jahrgang – Nummer 44 | 1. Dezember 1945

Nikolausabend

Durch die Nikolausnacht,
aus schneege[illegible]ugtem T[illegible]n,
klingelt ein Sch[illegible]itten;
knirrt ueber Steine,
und rumpelt ueber die Brueck[illegible]n.

Mitten auf der weissen weiten Heide
haelt er an.

Aus dem Himmel
schiesst goldener Glanz.
Hallende Harfen, jauchzende Engel,
herabregnende Holzpferdchen,
Schreipuppen, Trompeten,
Ruten und Marzipanh[illegible]en!

Lachend streicht sich Knecht Ruprecht
seinen langen Bruschebart.

Weiter trappelt der Hirsch,
der Stern vor seiner Stirn strahlt,
blau flimmert sein Atem.

Arno Holz

When the POWs were not working, numerous religious, recreational, and educational activities were available to them. One such activity included publishing the camp POW newsletters. Although generally published in German, they were occasionally printed in English as well. This POW newsletter was filled with drawings, puzzles, and articles. Educational activities were part of the US government's Intellectual Diversion Program, which was designed to educate POWs about the American way of life and—hopefully—increase their appreciation for it. Courses were available in over 30 different subjects, including English language and US history. (Both, Library of Congress.)

Members of this POW band entertained detainees with both German and American songs. The Geneva Convention governed POWs, who were under the supervision of American officers and civilians. While most of the men were content to abide by the rules and regulations, there were several successful escape attempts. Eventually, the escapees were caught or returned to Camp Forrest. (CFF.)

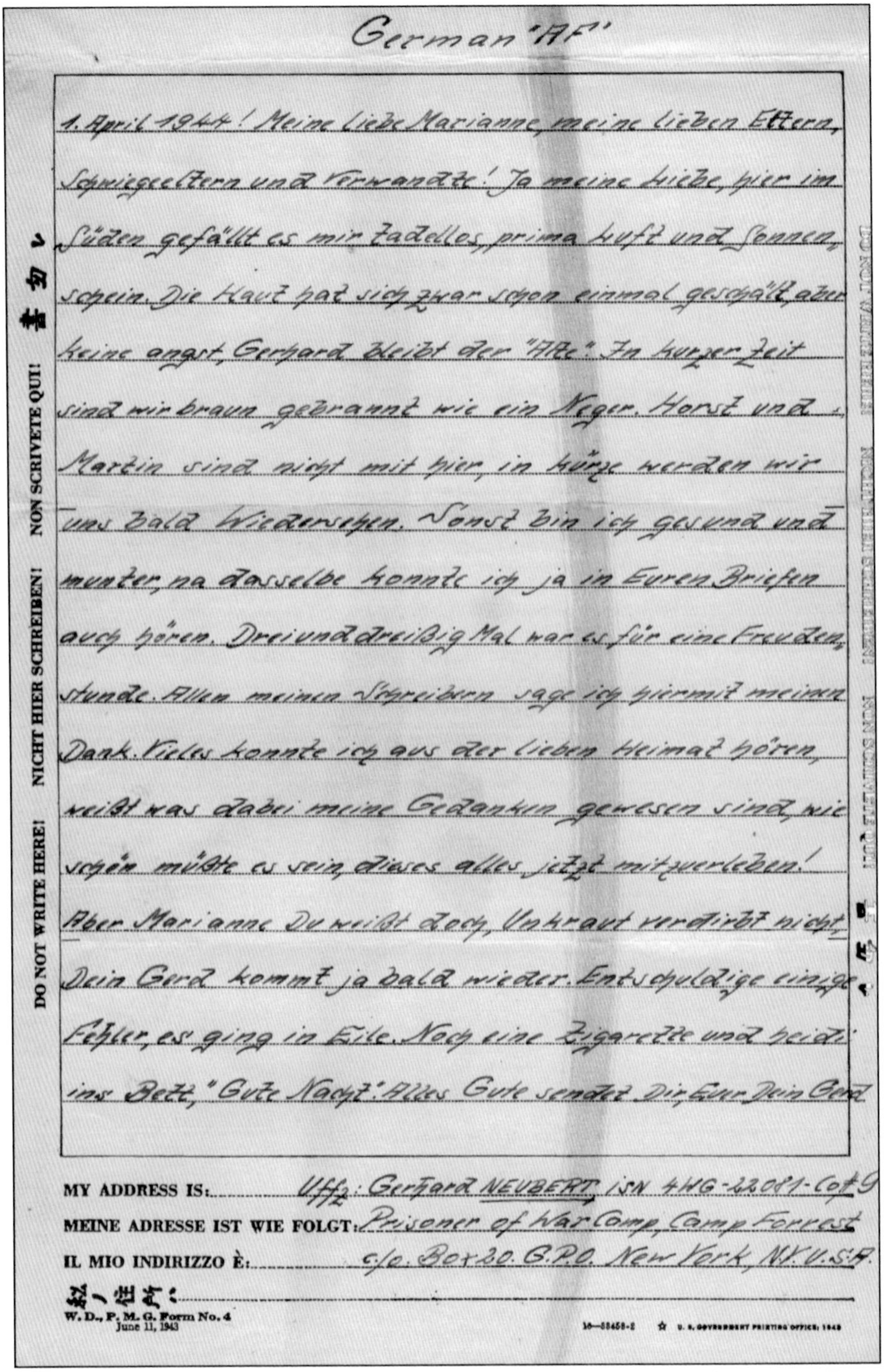
German "AF"

DO NOT WRITE HERE! NICHT HIER SCHREIBEN! NON SCRIVETE QUI!

1. April 1944! Meine liebe Marianne, meine lieben Eltern,
Schwiegereltern und Verwandte! Ja meine Liebe, hier im
Süden gefällt es mir tadellos, prima Luft und Sonnen-
schein. Die Haut hat sich zwar schon einmal geschält, aber
keine Angst, Gerhard bleibt der "Alte". In kurzer Zeit
sind wir braun gebrannt wie ein Neger. Horst und
Martin sind nicht mit hier, in Kürze werden wir
uns bald wiedersehen. Sonst bin ich gesund und
munter, na dasselbe konnte ich ja in Euren Briefen
auch hören. Dreiunddreißig Mal war es für eine Freuden-
stunde. Allen meinen Schreibern sage ich hiermit meinen
Dank. Vieles konnte ich aus der lieben Heimat hören,
weißt was dabei meine Gedanken gewesen sind, wie
schön müßte es sein, dieses alles jetzt mitzuerleben!
Aber Marianne Du weißt doch, Unkraut verdirbt nicht,
Dein Gerd kommt ja bald wieder. Entschuldige einige
Fehler, es ging in Eile. Noch eine Zigarette und heidi
ins Bett, "Gute Nacht". Alles Gute sendet Dir, Euer Dein Gerd

MY ADDRESS IS: Uffz: Gerhard NEUBERT, ISN 4WG-22081-Co.#9
MEINE ADRESSE IST WIE FOLGT: Prisoner of War Camp, Camp Forrest
IL MIO INDIRIZZO È: c/o. Box 20. G.P.O. New York, N.Y. U.S.A.

W. D., P. M. G. Form No. 4
June 11, 1943

16—35458-2 U. S. GOVERNMENT PRINTING OFFICE: 1943

In April 1944, German Air Force POW Gerhard Neubert sent this letter from Camp Forrest to his wife, Marianne Neubert, in Germany. In the letter, he indicates that he is doing well and that his wounds are healing slowly. He does not want his wife to worry, as one of his comrades is caring for the wounds. He remarks about the good weather in the South and how everyone is

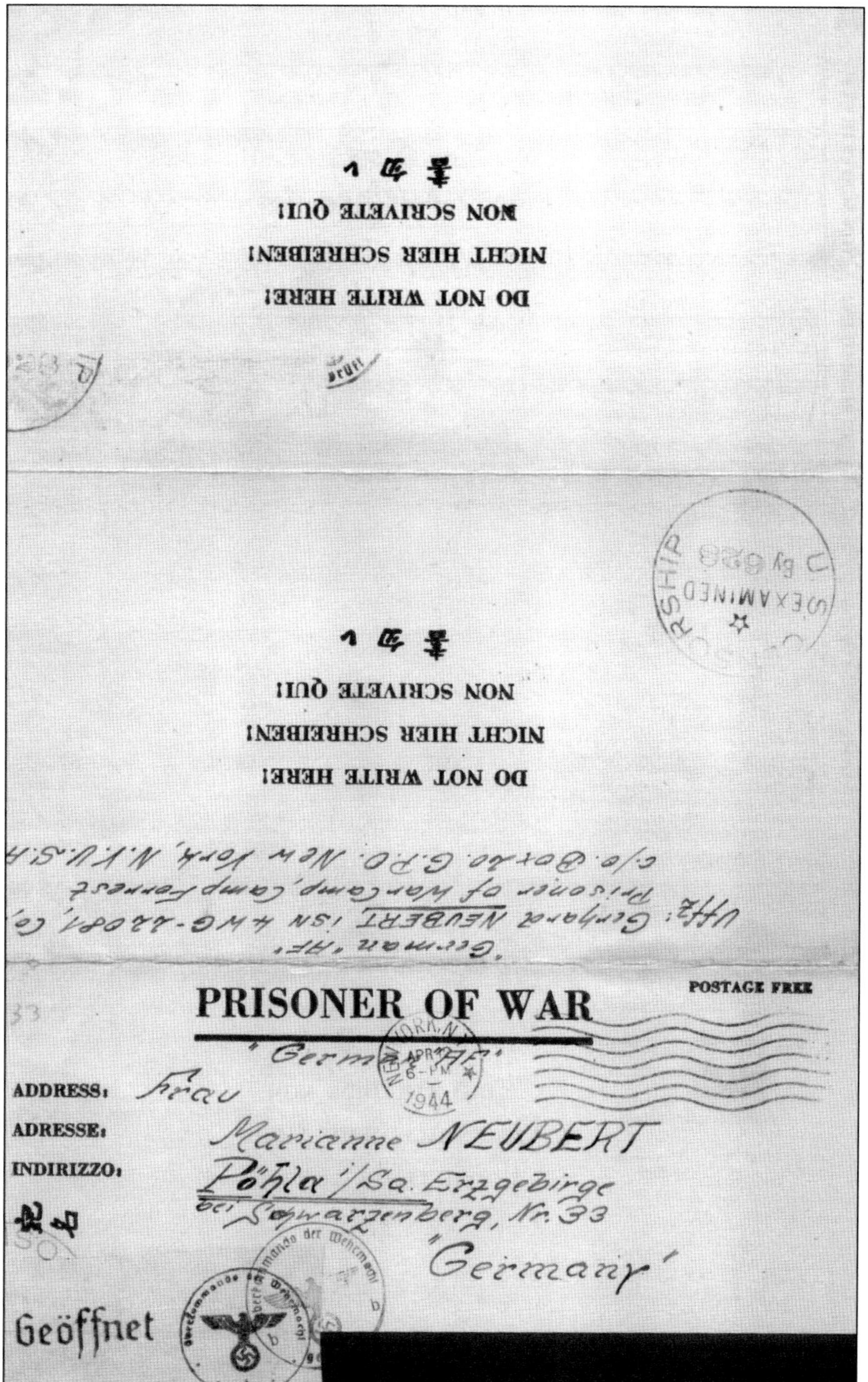

becoming quite tanned. He was glad to hear everyone was doing well at home, but he was very homesick. Her letters bring him much joy. He writes about how much he loves her and assures her he will be home soon. The letter does not mention any type of mistreatment by or ill will toward his captors. (Both, CFF.)

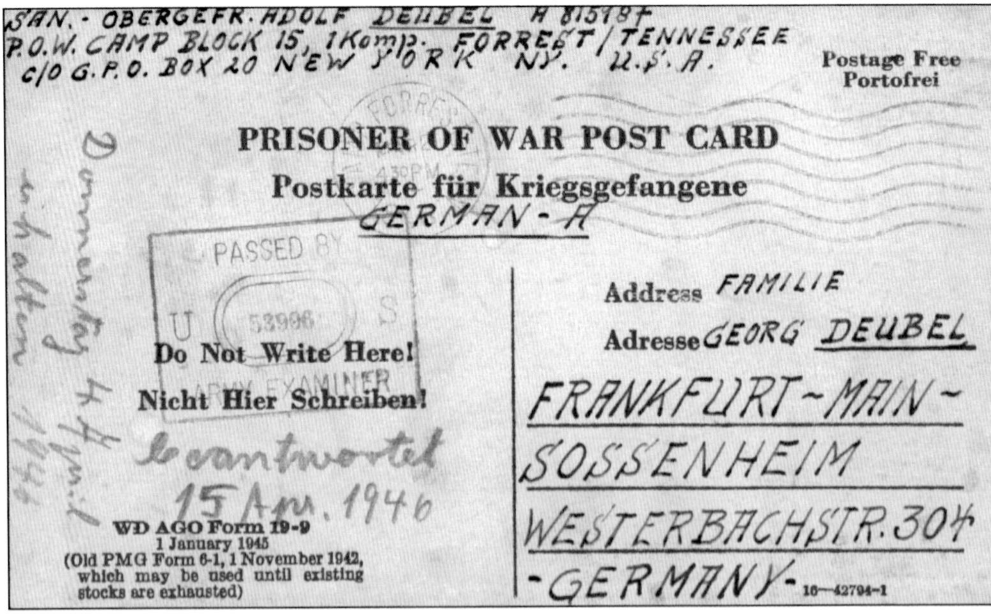

SAN. - OBERGEFR. ADOLF DEUBEL A 815187
P.O.W. CAMP BLOCK 15, 1Komp. FORREST / TENNESSEE
c/o G.P.O. BOX 20 NEW YORK NY. U.S.A.

Postage Free
Portofrei

PRISONER OF WAR POST CARD
Postkarte für Kriegsgefangene
GERMAN - A

PASSED BY
U 53996 S
ARMY EXAMINER

Do Not Write Here!
Nicht Hier Schreiben!

Donnerstag 4 April 1946 erhalten
beantwortet 15 Apr. 1946

WD AGO Form 19-9
1 January 1945
(Old PMG Form 6-1, 1 November 1942, which may be used until existing stocks are exhausted)

Address FAMILIE
Adresse GEORG DEUBEL
FRANKFURT-MAIN-
SOSSENHEIM
WESTERBACHSTR. 30¼
-GERMANY-

16—42794-1

German POWs wrote to and received letters from family and friends in their home country. Both American and German censors reviewed the postcards and letters to ensure that seditious information was not hidden within the text of a document or the stationery on which it was written. POW Adolf Deubel sent this postcard to his parents in Germany. He writes that he was excited to receive their letter and that he is happy and relieved to hear everyone there is healthy. He tells them he is healthy and not to worry about him. (Both, CFF.)

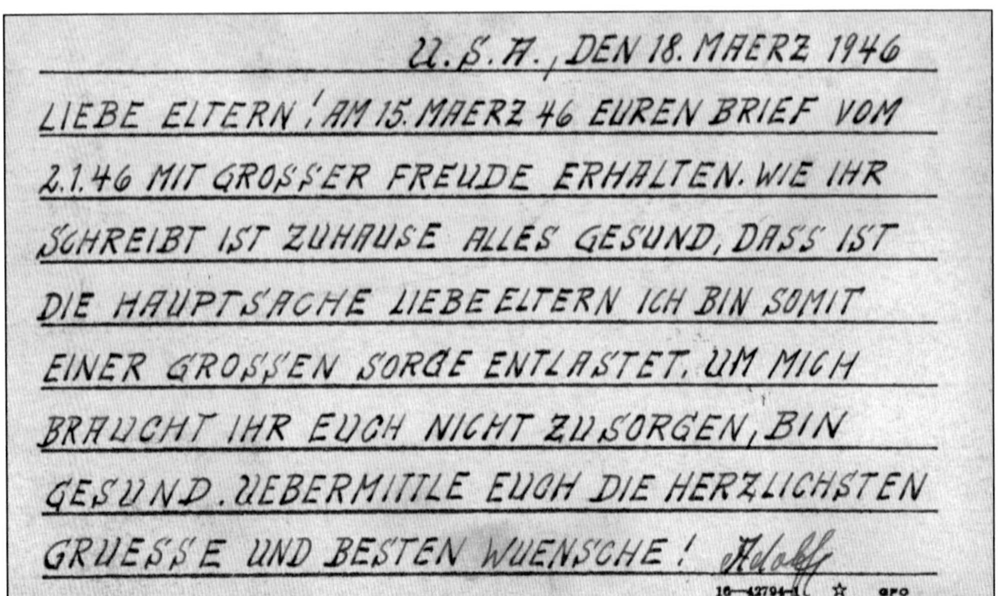

U.S.A., DEN 18. MAERZ 1946
LIEBE ELTERN! AM 15. MAERZ 46 EUREN BRIEF VOM
2.1.46 MIT GROSSER FREUDE ERHALTEN. WIE IHR
SCHREIBT IST ZUHAUSE ALLES GESUND, DASS IST
DIE HAUPTSACHE LIEBE ELTERN ICH BIN SOMIT
EINER GROSSEN SORGE ENTLASTET. UM MICH
BRAUCHT IHR EUCH NICHT ZU SORGEN, BIN
GESUND. UEBERMITTLE EUCH DIE HERZLICHSTEN
GRUESSE UND BESTEN WUENSCHE! Adolf

16—42794-1 ☆ GPO

These POWs were photographed unloading railcars at the train depot. The items being unloaded were used to build bridges. POWs were paid approximately 80¢ per day, which was mandated by the Geneva Convention. They could not work to produce military-related goods but were employed in a variety of labor positions in the logging and agriculture industries. Generally, guards were dispatched to ensure there were no escape attempts. The agriculture industry in the South routinely employed the POWs throughout the year, and farmers begged camp commanders to delay repatriation until after harvest season due to the tremendous labor shortages. (Both, CFF.)